FROM
NAZI TEST PILOT
TO
HITLER'S BUNKER

FROM NAZI TEST PILOT TO HITLER'S BUNKER

The Fantastic Flights of Hanna Reitsch

Dennis Piszkiewicz

Westport, Connecticut
London

Library of Congress Cataloging-in-Publication Data

Piszkiewicz, Dennis.
    From Nazi Test Pilot to Hitler's Bunker : the fantastic flights of Hanna
Reitsch / Dennis Piszkiewicz.
        p.   cm.
    Includes bibliographical references (p.   ) and index.
    ISBN 0-275-95456-0 (alk. paper)
        1. Reitsch, Hanna.   2. Women air pilots—Germany—Biography.
3. Air pilots, Military—Germany—Biography.   I. Title.
TL540.R38P57 1997
629.13'092—dc21
    [B]   97-11458

British Library Cataloguing in Publication Data is available.

Library of Congress Catalog Card Number: 97–11458
ISBN: 0-275-95456-0

First published in 1997

Praeger Publishers, 88 Post Road West, Westport, CT 06881
An imprint of Greenwood Publishing Group, Inc.

Printed in the United States of America

The paper used in this book complies with the
Permanent Paper Standard issued by the National
Information Standards Organization (Z39.48-1984).

10 9 8 7 6 5 4 3 2 1

For P. J.

Contents

Photographs follow pages 46 and 106.

Preface

Culture puts barriers in the paths of women who endeavor to excel. In many societies, it is rare for a woman to succeed. When one excels in a repressive culture—especially one repressive to women—it is remarkable. Thus, the story of Hanna Reitsch is amazing, and it would be inspirational had she not been a believer in Nazi Germany and a devoted friend of Adolf Hitler.

Hanna Reitsch was a young woman with a passion for flying. Her achievements as a pilot have often been given a quick summary in a list of gliding and soaring records she earned over a career that spanned the years from 1932 through 1978. By one account she set more than forty records for altitude and endurance in both gliders and powered aircraft.[1] Her real achievement as a pilot and a test pilot, however, was in squeezing the maximum performance out of a broad range of conventional, radically designed, and dangerous aircraft—and surviving. A summary of the most notable of these aircraft is given in Appendix A.

Hanna Reitsch had the drive of Amelia Earhart, the vision of Charles Lindbergh, and the daring of Chuck Yeager. Though she

earned a place for herself in history as a pilot, she was, regrettably
and inexplicably, devoted to the Nazi cause. She is now better known
as a witness to the last days of the Third Reich than as an extraordinary pilot. In the end, she paid tragically for her association with
the Nazis.

Hanna Reitsch did some extraordinary things in an environment
that gave her few opportunities and less encouragement. From the
very beginning, Nazi policy expelled women from positions of political and public influence; it restricted them to the roles of childbearers
and poorly paid laborers in the most menial jobs.[2] German women
who surmounted these barriers during the twelve years of Hitler's
rule are remarkably few. Scholars of the era would have trouble nam-
ing more than a handful of women—other than the nonachieving
wives and mistresses of Nazi leaders—who made their marks among
the thousands of male criminals, psychopaths, and social misfits who
dominated Nazi Germany.

So why did Hanna Reitsch stand out? Why couldn't she accept her
designated role of wife and breeder of future members of the master
race? What drove her to excel in a male-dominated world as an aircraft test pilot? What led her to become a close associate of the Nazi
leadership and, in the end, an intimate member of Hitler's inner circle? Couldn't she see that she was serving the devil?

The perspective of over fifty years makes our vision of the evil of
the Third Reich shockingly clear. But to a young woman whose entire
upbringing and education had been directed at making her a wife and
mother, the political truth may not have been obvious. Hanna Reitsch
knew no other culture or society. She had no other place or time in
which to express her identity and ambitions. She found in the Nazi
establishment opportunities and rewards for her achievements. Con-
sorting with the devil paid well; yet, in the end, Hanna Reitsch was
called on to pay back more than she had received. Her story shows
how hard it is for a woman to excel in a repressive society, and how
easy it is to follow a path that leads to hell.

Acknowledgments

I found the threads that came together to weave the story of Hanna Reitsch through many fine institutions. I thank the staffs of the following for their help: the Orange County Public Library, the Los Angeles County Public Library, the library of the Simon Wiesenthal Center in Los Angeles, and the library of the University of California at Irvine. Additionally, I thank the staffs of the Air and Space Museum of the Smithsonian Institution, and the Library of Congress. I owe special thanks for locating photographs to the staffs of the National Archives Still Pictures Branch and to the National Air and Space Museum of the Smithsonian Institution.

Not surprisingly, many women encouraged me to tell the story of Hanna Reitsch with all of its good, bad, and horrific details. For their support in the forms of suggestions, criticism, and the grim job of proofreading, I especially thank P. J. Kaylor, Lyn Chevli, and Wilma Kaylor.

I also thank Marvin Kaylor, pilot and engineer, for keeping my writing technically correct; and I thank Dan Eades, my editor, for his faith in this project and his encouragement.

FROM
NAZI TEST PILOT
TO
HITLER'S BUNKER

Honor

26 April 1945

The woman in the cramped seat behind the pilot savored the serenity of dusk, knowing that in a few moments the enemy would try to kill them. She noticed, below their small plane, the silver shimmer of light from the tranquil waters of the Wannsee. Above them, she knew, Russian fighters were everywhere, ready to dive upon them like hawks on a lost sparrow if they gave away their presence. The ground ahead was also controlled by the enemy, promising a passage through a deadly gauntlet.

Only minutes earlier, they had taken off from the encircled airport at Gatow on a desperate mission to the center of the city, which was also besieged by the enemy. The man had insisted on being at the controls, citing his experience of flying through enemy fire as a combat pilot. She was with him, they agreed, because only she could pick out the landmarks that would guide them to their destination, though they both knew that their reasoning was only part of the truth.

The slow, single-engine plane with a broad wing above its cockpit crossed over the Grunewald. It was almost low enough to touch the fresh spring foliage of the ancient trees. The woman caught images of tanks, soldiers swarming among the trees, faces of Russian soldiers who shouldered their weapons and aimed at them. The pilot, in the seat in front of her, twisted the plane through exploding shells and bullets flying up haphazardly from the ground.

She saw a bright yellow flame smash into the plane and heard the pilot scream that he was hit. He was bleeding, fainting, and the airplane was out of control. The woman reached over his shoulder and grabbed the control stick. Shells burst around them in lethal puffs. The din of the explosions drowned out the roar of the airplane's small engine. The woman struggled at the controls, zigzagging it through the ground fire just above the treetops. Then the plane was hit again. The woman saw in horror that gasoline was pouring out through bullet holes punched in both wing tanks. She expected an explosion at any second.

The pilot stirred, reached for the control stick, then fell back into unconsciousness.

The woman recognized a radio tower poking through the smoke that billowed up from the burning city, and she knew that she was on course. The ground fire and bursting shells faded behind them, and the woman thought that the ground below might not yet have fallen to the enemy. The sulphurous clouds blocked out her view. She guided the plane by the compass, east, toward the center of the city, toward the ack-ack tower, a landmark she remembered.

Soon she saw below her a broad roadway that ran east-west through the city. She followed it over blocks of city that had been bombed to rubble. Then the Tiergarten appeared, the city's central park. She guided the plane past the Victory Monument at its center and glided down to the East-West Axis. They might still complete their mission if she could miss the craters in the roadway, if the gasoline pouring from the wing tanks did not ignite, if she could bring the plane to a stop before it reached the Brandenburg Gate.[1]

They keep asking her endless variations of the question, Where is Adolf Hitler? Is he dead or is he not dead? Looking at her, you would think her to be among the least likely to have the answers. At thirty-three, she is relatively young. Her stature is best described as diminutive; at five feet and one-half inch tall, she weighs barely a hundred pounds. Looking at her face, you might find her almost pretty. Her blue eyes are bright and lively. Her smile—when she smiles—is broad, possibly a little too broad. But she is in no mood to smile. Her nose wants to have a cutely upturned tip but seems flat and broad like that of a prizefighter who didn't duck a punch.

The interrogator puts pen to paper and records his observations:

8 October 1945

SUMMARY OF INTERROGATION
THE LAST DAYS IN HITLER'S AIR RAID SHELTER

Source:

Name: Fraulein Hanna Reitsch.

Rank: Flugkapiten [Captain of the Air-Honorary title given for outstanding aeronautical achievement].

Date of birth: 29 March 1912.

Marital Status: Single.

Occupation: Test-pilot and aeronautical research expert.

Citizenship: German.

Address: Leopolds Krone Castle, Salzburg, Austria.

Political Status: Non-party member.

Decorations: Iron Cross first class.[2]

She speaks, and it is with an intensity that startles you. She says everything she feels, deliberately yet with difficulty, as if she must think out every emotion and idea from scratch. She is a true believer in a corrupt and dead cause. She has lost everything and everyone she values. She is a prisoner wanting freedom but with nowhere to go. She is confused now, but all of her passion is still there.

The interrogator continues to write:

> Her story is remarkable only in that she played a small part in the events of the War's end and that she had personal contact with the top-bracket Nazis as that end descended upon them. It is also of interest as it is likely that Reitsch is one of the last, if not the very last person who got out of the shelter alive. Her information is evaluated as reliable and it is possible that her story may throw some light on or perhaps serve as an aid to a fuller knowledge of what

happened during the last days of Berlin and of the War.

It will be noted that much of the report concerns itself with the Nazi and German interpretation of "honor." Reitsch herself, in answering queries, carefully weighs the "honor" aspects of every remark and then gives her answers carefully but truthfully. The use of the word amounts practically to a fetish complex with the source and is almost an incongruous embodiment of her entire philosophy. Her constant repetition of the word is in no manner as obvious to her as it is to the interrogator, nor is the meaning the same, nor does she recognize the incongruous use she makes of the word. . . .

She tells her story in conversational form, and although it is, in part, reproduced in that manner here, no pretense is made that the quotations are in all cases exact; they are simply given as she remembers them. If it is kept in mind that this material is a statement of her own opinions and observations, the information may be considered as completely reliable.[3]

The interrogator follows these observations with a retelling of the events that brought Hanna Reitsch to Berlin in the last few days before the Third Reich was swept from the earth. Hers is the story of a descent into hell and a last chance at redemption, which was given to her, ironically and unintentionally, by the ranking devil of the century, Adolf Hitler. In summing up, the interrogator writes:

She claims that the only reason she remained alive is for the sake of the truth; to tell the truth about Goering, "the shallow showman," to tell the truth about Hitler, "the criminal incompetent," and to tell the German people the truth about the dangers of the form of government that the Third Reich gave them. She believes that she is fulfilling much of that mission when she speaks to the interrogator. It is therefore felt that her remarks may be considered as her deepest efforts at sincerity and honesty. At the moment she is undergoing a severe mental struggle in an effort to reconcile her conception of "honor" with her denunciations of Goering, of Himmler, and of Hitler himself.[4]

After she had lost everything, after she had shed her loyalties to the leaders of the Third Reich, all she could still claim as her own—incomprehensible though it might have been—was her honor. Though honor was a silk-thin thread, she climbed it like a rope out of the pit of despair and madness.

But would the thread be strong enough to hold her, or would it break, casting her back into the abyss?

Chapter 1

Soaring over Silesia

Why would anybody want to fly? Why would a young girl, born in the second decade of the century and bred by her middle-class parents to be a wife and mother, want to take up the highly impractical and, at that time, clearly dangerous activity of getting into a primitive machine and leaving the safety of the earth? If you have to ask, perhaps you would not understand.

Hanna Reitsch, the child, watched as storks crossed the azure sky above her native Silesia in stately, steady flight. Buzzards circled and soared with the updrafts fired by the summer sun. With every bird that passed overhead, Hanna dreamed that she could fly with it. In the innocence of childhood, all dreams are possible.[1]

The young science of aviation was maturing. Aircraft were becoming more sophisticated and reliable, though they still might turn on the unprepared pilot. World War I had been the impetus for accelerated development, and in the following years, they were being viewed more and more as a mode of civil transportation.

Though people of all nations seemed to be flying, taking greater risks, and setting records for distance and speed between widely separated points on earth, Germans were less likely to leave the earth or fly beyond their borders. The Treaty of Versailles denied Germany an air force, effectively stripping it of an aircraft industry and any vehicles capable of long-distance flight. German flying enthusiasts were stuck with whatever they could cobble together from World I's leftovers and materials they could acquire with their meager assets. Motors were usually beyond reach. Unpowered gliders became the German standard.

Pilots were as brave as ever, and their exploits brought them instant fame. In May 1927 Charles Lindbergh piloted his single-engine aircraft from New York to Paris, thereby becoming an instant international celebrity. In June of the following year, a young American pilot named Amelia Earhart became the first woman to cross the Atlantic by air, albeit as a passenger. In 1930 an English woman named Amy Johnson flew solo from England to Australia. Hanna was, no doubt, aware of the exploits of these early pioneers of aviation and also of the fact that many of these pilots were women, although she never related her direction in life to their accomplishments.[2]

Every now and then, a man-made craft sailed above Silesia. It would be a glider from Grunau, a town perched on the side of a mountain called the Galgenberg, where there was a school for glider pilots. Grunau was a short bicycle ride from Hanna's home in Hirschberg. When she was in her mid-teens, Hanna told her father that someday she wanted to fly. Hanna's father was a practical man. He wanted her to get this nonsense out of her adolescent head and focus on the reality of her current education. He made a deal with her. If she would not mention flying until she had completed her secondary education, he would, as a reward, let her take the course for glider pilots. He expected her to forget about their deal. Whenever she could, Hanna would pedal her bicycle to Grunau to enviously watch the students go through their exercises on the slopes of the Galgenberg.[1]

The Reitsch family was firmly anchored in the values of the middle class and German tradition. Its patriarch, Dr. Willy Reitsch was a native of Silesia. Though Frau Emy Reitsch's family came from the Austrian Tyrol, she shared her husband's German culture and tended to the home and children. Frau Emy Reitsch gave birth to her second child, Hanna, on 29 March 1912. Hanna had two siblings: her brother Kurt, who was two years older, and sister Heidi, two years younger.[3]

Hanna painted her mother with words of unequaled praise:

I cannot remember her otherwise than sweet-tempered and calm of spirit. To us children, she was what, in their hearts, all mothers would wish to be, patient, consoling, edifying, and tireless, but she also possessed the gift, not given to all mothers, of making us aware of her love and as a consequence our lives were wonderfully enriched.

The bond between mother and daughter was unusually close. Emy Reitsch was the constant guiding light in her daughter's life. She was the force that calmed the impulsive girl. She was the constant counselor to the adult woman until the final days of World War II. Emy Reitsch wrote to her every day during her flying career, though Hanna might be in another country or on another continent. In the turmoil that would come, Emy Reitsch would be at her daughter's side with aid and comfort, steadying her through her times of crisis.

In her autobiography, Hanna had surprisingly little to say about her father and his impact on her direction in life. Perhaps this spare telling of the facts reflected her reaction to events that transpired at the end of World War II.

Dr. Willy Reitsch was an ophthalmologist and head of a private eye-clinic in Hirschberg. His office was on the first floor of the Reitsch residence. Hanna remembered her father as being strict in both moral and material matters. Even though his family was comfortably middle class and had a family maid, his children, Hanna recalled, were deprived of sweets and chocolates even when offered as gifts from her father's patients. From the perspective given by time, one might conclude him to be authoritarian; however, he may have been no more so than the average middle-class German father of his time.[4]

Willy Reitsch was not necessarily a cold person; he clearly loved his children and involved himself in their education, though on a more academic level than did their mother. Even when his children were very young, he would take Hanna and her older brother Kurt, in turns, on his daily rounds at the eye clinic. He took delight in obtaining animal eyes from the butcher to show his children the anatomy of the eye and simple surgical procedures. Not surprisingly, Hanna developed an interest in medicine, even though as a girl she was expected to follow her mother's example into a domestic life.[1]

After his medical practice and his family, Willy Reitsch's great interest was music. He would play his cello daily, often between appointments with patients and for a quarter of an hour before midday meals. When he did join his family to eat, his children would often greet him with a Tyrolean yodel—learned from their mother—which would invariably bring a smile to his face.[4]

Religious matters in the Reitsch family, like the raising of children and the management of domestic issues, were the domain of Emy Reitsch. Willy Reitsch was a Protestant; his wife was a Catholic. They had agreed that the children would be raised as Protestants; however, the patriarch of the Reitsch clan did not practice his religion openly and left the religious upbringing of his children to his wife. The result of this agreement was that Emy Reitsch taught her children her simple faith. Emy's constant messages to her children, especially Hanna, were faith in God and humility.[5]

As a child, Hanna was adventuresome, impulsive, and a bit of a tomboy, no doubt inspired by her older brother, Kurt. Her enthusiasm overflowed in a flood of words, superlatives, and snap judgments. Energy of this kind in a child is normal, and Emy Reitsch tried to guide and temper it. When Hanna was six years old, her mother taught her an exercise that would serve her well later in life. After the midday meal, Emy Reitsch had her children, Kurt and Hanna, stretch out on the floor with their hands behind their heads, their eyes closed, and nothing on their minds for five minutes. Hanna could not figure out how to think of nothing for a few seconds, much less five minutes. She resorted to a prayer asking God to help her think of nothing, which she repeated until her five minutes were up. She turned the exercise in relaxation into one of focus and concentration.[6]

As she grew older, Hanna saw in herself a need for discipline. It was a practical issue, too. If she wanted to fly, she would have to live up to her bargain with her father not to mention flying until she completed her schooling; and this—as her father could undoubtedly see—would be the ultimate act of self-discipline. Hanna took guidance from a book she came across, the *Meditations* of Ignatius Loyola. Loyola, a leader in the Counter-Reformation and founder of the Jesuits, had devised a set of exercises intended to remove spiritual faults by means of self-examination. She knew she was making progress when her mother commented on her growing maturity.

In 1930 Hanna completed her secondary education. Her father

wanted to celebrate the event by presenting her with an antique gold watch. Hanna declined the gift and reminded him of his promise to let her learn to fly. Dr. Willy Reitsch would live up to his promise.

Before Hanna began her flying lessons and before she entered medical school, her parents wanted her to attend a school of domestic science—a finishing school for young women—for one year. If her career plans did not work out or if she met the right man, she would then have the skills she would need to fall back on to become a wife and mother. Hanna left with little enthusiasm for the Colonial School for Women—an anachronism since Germany gave up its colonies at the end of the First World War. Hanna's first remarkable experience in an unremarkable year was a holiday break in which she was free to take her first flying lesson.[7]

Hanna Reitsch arrived for her first flying lesson at the Grunau Training School for glider pilots in the latter part of 1930. She rode her bicycle from her home in Hirschberg to the Galgenberg as she had done so many times before. There she met her classmates, all young men, and the instructor, a man named Pit van Husen.

At the age of nineteen, she was, by most standards, a grown woman. Yet, her diminutive stature belied the fact. At five feet and one half-inch tall, she weighed no more than ninety pounds. She was a blue-eyed blonde with sharp features and an enthusiastic smile. Hanna was moderately attractive, in a pixieish way, but thoroughly unimpressive as a potential pilot.

The first exercise was to practice balance. An aircraft, especially a glider, will go in whatever direction the center of gravity shifts. To fly it steady, the balance must be centered. At Grunau, the student would sit in the cockpit of a rudimentary, open-cockpit glider, the Grunau 9, while the instructor van Husen steadied the craft by holding a wing tip. When he let go, the student had to balance the craft by adjusting the control stick to move the balance, just as they would have to do in flight. Hanna took her turn and succeeded, as eventually did all of the students.

The next exercise was to control the motion of the glider as it slid down the meadow. The student was to balance the glider, as before, by adjusting the ailerons, and to keep it traveling in a straight line by using the foot pedals, which controlled the rudder. Hanna sat in the glider cockpit as her fellow students attached a rubber shock cord, a "bunje" as they called it, to the hook on the nose of the glider. The shock cord divided into two at its other end; and two groups of four men each, standing some distance in front of the glider, held these two branches. Another group was behind the glider, holding onto its tail. The plan was for the men in front to move forward, stretching the rubber shock cord as far as it would go. The men at the tail would then let go. The glider with Hanna at the controls would snap forward like a stone out of a slingshot. All Hanna had to do was guide the glider along a straight course, keeping the wings level, as it slid down the meadow. The glider was not to leave the ground.

The instructor began the chant that preceded action by shouting, "Heave!" The men in front of the glider began walking, stretching the long shock cords forward.

The instructor shouted, "Double!" The men ran forward stretching the shock cord as far as it would go.

Suppose, Hanna wondered, when the glider began to move, she pulled back on the stick, just a fraction, no more than six or seven inches. What if she lifted the glider off the ground, not far, just a yard or so?

"Away!" The men holding the tail let go, and the glider snapped forward. Hanna's head snapped back, and, whether it was reaction or will, she pulled back on the stick.

All she could see was sky. She was airborne, though she did not know how high.

She heard the shouts from the ground, "Down! Down!" So she pushed the stick forward, and down she went.

The ground raced up at her, and she pulled the stick back before the earth could smash her. Then down, then up again, then the glider lost its air speed, and there was no more going up. The glider crashed, her safety straps tore apart, and Hanna was thrown out of the cockpit. Luckily, both Hanna and the glider were unharmed.

Everybody was running down the hill toward her. Her classmates were yelling insults at her. The instructor, Pit van Husen, was yelling too. What had she tried to do? She could have killed herself; and, worse yet, she could have destroyed the glider. She was disobedient and undisciplined. She was unfit to be a pilot.

"As a punishment," the instructor shouted at her, "you will be grounded for three days!"

Her classmates christened her "Stratosphere," a nickname she kept for the remainder of the course. The instructor, Pit van Husen and

Wolf Hirth, head of the Grunau Training School debated kicking Hanna out before she killed someone—possibly herself. Luckily for Hanna, they put off their decision.[8]

That night Hanna locked herself in her room at home in Hirschberg and admitted the truth to herself: She had bungled her first opportunity in a cockpit. She had been undisciplined and had disobeyed her trainer's instructions with nearly tragic results. She resolved that she would never again disobey instructions. Never.

Even if she could discipline herself to obey orders, there was still the matter of controlling the glider. Hanna fell back on the lessons in relaxation and concentration taught to her as a child by her mother, and on the exercises of self-mastery taught by Ignatius Loyola. She sat on her bed holding a walking stick between her knees as if it were the control stick of the aircraft. Her eyes were closed, and she imagined that she was in the cockpit again on the high mountain meadow. In her mind she heard the instructor shout, "Heave! Double! Away!", as he had done earlier that day, and she imagined feeling the glider snap forward down the gentle slope. Control. She moved the stick gently, balancing the glider as it slid, keeping the wing tips level until it came to a smooth stop. For more than an hour she imagined guiding the glider on its slide down the meadow. She stopped only when she was sure, in her imagination, that she could succeed at this simple exercise. Then she began to pull back gently on the stick, lifting the glider off the ground in short, controlled hops.

Hanna spent the next two days helping to haul the glider up the hill after the other students' practices, putting up with their verbal abuse, and watching. She watched everything they did, learning from their successes and their mistakes. Finally, on the third day, she was allowed to sit at the controls. Her observation of her classmates and her nighttime practices served her well. She performed the regulation downhill slides and short hops satisfactorily; and, before long, her skills were on a par with those of her classmates. To pass the glider course for beginners, students were required to pass the "A" test by keeping the glider airborne over a straight course for thirty seconds. The first student to take the "A" test was a plump, middle-aged man. The lack of wind that day, combined with his considerable weight, kept him earthbound. The instructor told Hanna to get into the glider where it had come to rest, part way down the grassy slope. He expected her to take another short, harmless slide down what was left of the slope.

"Heave! Double! Away!" The glider was airborne with the ninety-pound girl at the controls. Hanna fixed her sight on the horizon and kept the wings level. She was still above the ground, gliding through the air, sinking slowly as the ground below her also sloped away. At last the tiny craft touched down. She guided it on a straight course till it came to a stop, and the left wing tip slowly dipped to touch the ground. Hanna had been airborne for thirty-nine seconds, nine more than required to pass the "A" test.

The instructor said, "I expect that was just luck. I can't count it for your 'A' Test. You had better try again, straight away."

Hanna could not believe what she heard, but maybe the instructor was right. Maybe her thirty-nine-second flight was just a fluke. Before her doubts grew enough to paralyze her, she was airborne again. Her flight was straight and long. It was not just luck: "Test passed."[9]

Two days later Hanna began to prepare for the "B" test. It required that the student fly a course of S-turns. After Hanna's remarkable improvement, Wolf Hirth, head of the school, took an interest in her. He apparently saw in her an intensity and potential that made her stand out from her fellow students. Hirth began with Hanna by giving her personal lessons on how to guide a glider through various turns. Hanna practiced at night with her walking stick and by day in a glider. When the day of the "B" test came, she passed it on the first try.[10]

Hanna returned to the Colonial School for Women to complete her course. By her account, her single major accomplishment that year was to housebreak the pigs the school raised for food. She taught them to use one of two adjoining pigsties as a dining and sitting room and to use the other as a toilet.[7]

In the spring of 1931, six months after her first gliding lessons, she returned to the Grunau Training School for the advanced course that would let her take the "C" test.

A wind was blowing from the west, sliding across the low meadows then up the side of the Galgenberg and over its top. The shape of the mountain forced the wind upward, and it carried anything that rode the wind, like buzzards and gliders, up into the sky.

The glider used in the "C" course was of a more sophisticated design than that used in the beginners' course; it had an enclosed cockpit and sleek fuselage. The glider was on the high slope of the Galgenberg where a group of students was taking turns at the "C" test. To pass the "C" test, the students had to fly the glider for at least five minutes above the starting height. They had to catch the air currents rising along the western slope of the mountain and, by reversing their course back and forth along the mountain's face, ride the wind into the sky. Wolf Hirth, head of the gliding school, personally coached Hanna on how to pass the "C" test.[11]

"All ready? Heave! Double! Away!"

With the familiar chant, the glider with Hanna at its controls jerked into motion and was airborne.

Hanna turned the plane to the right to parallel the slope, and immediately she felt the rising wind lift the glider. She climbed higher and higher and felt as if she were flying like a bird. She followed the ridge to the far end where, according to instructions, she turned into the wind and reversed her course along the mountain. The ridge of the mountain was already drifting far below her, and she could see just below it the starting site and her fellow students. Again she turned into the wind and retraced her course above the broad shoulder of the mountain.

Suddenly, she saw two dark spots drifting with the wind ahead of her and at the same altitude: buzzards. The glider was moving faster than the birds, and Hanna tried to catch up with them. She got close enough to see their dark feathers; but the buzzards, wary of their bigger sister, soared higher on the rising wind. Hanna turned the glider to find the up wind and chase the dark birds. She chased her winged brothers higher and higher, lost in the joy and freedom of the sky.

Hanna looked at her wristwatch. She had been flying for over twenty minutes. To pass the "C" test, she had to be airborne five minutes; she was allowed a maximum of ten because other students would need time in the glider to take their tests. The instructor and her fellow students were, no doubt, angry with her; and there would be hell to pay. Unless . . .

According to her instructions, she was to land the glider on the broad meadow at the foot of the mountain. The students would then take about half an hour to haul it up the slope so that the next student could take the "C" test. Hanna wondered if she should land the glider near the top of the mountain at the exact point where the next student would take off. The time needed to bring the plane back up the mountain would be saved, and no harm would have been done by her extended flight. She quickly lost height and positioned herself above the takeoff site on the upper slope, then she pushed the control stick forward.

On the ground below, Wolf Hirth and the other students watched in horror as they saw the glider diving toward them, then horror turned to anger at the girl who was about to wreck the glider and the other students' chances to earn their "C" certificates. Just above the ground the tiny craft leveled off, touched down, and slid to the exact spot Hanna had been aiming at.

"I ought really to be angry with you for acting against instructions," Hirth said to Hanna, "and as a warning to the rest of you, I will repeat here and now: Anyone who acts in [the] future in this way without first obtaining permission, will be grounded at once. We must have discipline here." Then Hirth added, "From the flying point of view, the performance was perfect."

Hanna had broken her resolution to never again disobey instructions. In the process, she learned that if she acted with style and flair, not only could she get away with her transgressions, she could also profit by them. A few days after she passed the "C" test, Hirth gave Hanna permission to fly the school's new glider, a privilege that would normally be reserved for the head of the school and its instructors. Hanna Reitsch was on her way to becoming the darling of the German skies.[12]

Hanna's experience at Grunau exhibited a pattern that marked her career and her professional experiences with men until the end of the Third Reich. She took a step up, reaching beyond her experience; and she was viewed by many—if not most—of the men who dominated the skies as being out of place. Many did not take her seriously. Others viewed her as an intruder into an all male club. Countering this negative experience, she found—or was found—by one man, older and more experienced, who saw promise in her. He would become her mentor and professional guardian until she met another man of higher position who could offer her more opportunities and challenges. Wolf Hirth became the first of many mentors.

When her glorious summer of flying ended, Hanna went to Berlin to begin her first term in medical school; but her mind was still on flying. She learned that the German Air Mails ran a flying school at Staaken, in the western suburbs of Berlin. She convinced her parents that for her to become a flying missionary doctor as she now dreamed, she would have to master powered flight. Before long, she was setting off on her bicycle at 5:00 A.M. for Staaken and her flying lessons. When weather conditions kept the students grounded, Hanna spent her time in the workshops watching the mechanics and learning about engines as well as aircraft. The mechanics tacitly accepted her as one of their own after she demonstrated her mechanical ability by dismantling an old engine and then spending a long weekend reassembling it.[13]

Her experience flying gliders helped her to quickly master the controls of a powered aircraft. After only a few flights with an instructor, she soloed. Not long after that, she took her altitude test. Bundled in a fur-lined flying suit, she piloted an old Mercedes-Klemm with an anemic twenty-horsepower engine to an altitude of 6,500 feet. She felt, she said, as if she were close to God. Her mind was clear and quiet. Pride, she said, dissolved into humility in the vastness of the sky. But when she returned to earth, her pride also returned.[14]

Spring of 1932 held inspiring news for any young woman who wanted to fly. On 22 and 23 May, five years to the day after Charles Lindbergh flew from New York to Paris, a young American woman named Amelia Earhart flew her single-engine Vega across the Atlantic, from Newfoundland to Ireland. It was, in fact, Earhart's second crossing of the Atlantic by air. In 1928 she had been aboard the trimotor seaplane that had a two-man crew and herself as a passenger.[15] On this, her second crossing, Earhart was the first woman to pilot an aircraft solo across the ocean, and she did it in record time.[16]

To what extent Hanna allowed herself to be inspired by Amelia Earhart, she never said; but in the summer of 1932 she returned to Grunau with her usual intense enthusiasm for flying. During the year Hanna had spent in Berlin, Wolf Hirth and his wife had become friends with her parents; and the Reitsches agreed that their daughter could devote her summer to flying, provided that she continued her medical studies in the fall. In the three summer months of 1932, Hanna again received personal flying instructions from Wolf Hirth, an experience that would form the basis of her later career.[17]

During this idyllic summer, Hanna met a young man named Wernher von Braun, who was also taking an advanced gliding course at Grunau.[18] It was inevitable that the tall, young son of an aristocrat and the diminutive girl with the infectious smile and well-developed sense of daring would become lifelong friends. Both were ambitious dreamers. Hanna talked of becoming a missionary doctor who flew to her charges, and Wernher wanted to fly into space. That year, young Wernher would receive his license to fly powered aircraft and also his bachelor's degree from the Berlin Institute of Technology.

In the fall, von Braun would go to work for the German army, where he would create an amazing and terrifying rocket.[19]

In the fall, Hanna reluctantly returned to her medical studies. Doctor Willy Reitsch sent his daughter for her second term in medical school to the University at Kiel, where he had received part of his education and where there were no sport aviation facilities to distract her. To Hanna's shock and chagrin, there was an overabundance of students at Kiel, and the faculty winnowed down the ranks of those entering the second term with an oral entrance exam. Hanna was terrified by the prospect of the exam and certain that she would fail, having learned nothing about medicine during her first term in Berlin. When her turn came, she was asked by the examining professor to discuss the anatomy of the thigh, and she was saved from failure and disgrace, ironically, by Wolf Hirth.[20]

In his youth, Hirth had lost a leg in a motorcycle accident.[21] In accord with his agreement with her parents' wishes that she study medicine, Hirth insisted that she make a presentation to him about the anatomy of his injury, the knee and the thigh. Hanna repeated what she had learned for her flying instructor to the professor at Kiel, and she passed the oral exam. Whether she liked it or not, she would spend another year studying to be a doctor.[20]

As Hanna Reitsch was finding her place in the skies above Germany, political changes that would affect all Germans were also taking place. In the election of 5 March 1933, the Nazi party won a 44 percent minority representation in the Reichstag. The Nazis quickly went about eliminating their rivals and solidifying their position. Adolf Hitler became Chancellor, and a new order was in control of Germany. Change brought harm to some and advantages to others.[22] Those who were of a democratic mind, political opponents of the Nazis, and, of course, the Jews were in for a very rough time. Those who supported the new regime and the program it embarked on would profit from it. Hanna Reitsch would find that the Nazi regime would boost her career, then overpower her life.

Chapter 2

Flight Instructor to Test Pilot

The early days of unpowered flight were ones of gliding. The over-sized kites would be carried to the top of a hill, and with the pilot aboard, they would be snapped into the air and glide to a lower level. The Americans introduced the use of tow planes to lift the gliders to altitude,[1] but the principle was the same. The glider was the slave of gravity and would quickly reach the ground. Gravity could be beaten if a pilot could find a rising wind. A breeze blowing against a mountain ridge, such as the Galgenberg where Grunau was located, could supply lift; but it would keep a glider aloft only as long as the glider flew above the rising terrain.

It was obvious to pilots who watched the sky that there were other invisible currents of rising air. Eagles and buzzards found them and sailed high into the sky on *thermals*. A *thermal* is a column of air rising because it has been heated by sunlight striking the ground below it. How thermals are formed and how to exploit them to fly an unpowered aircraft were mysteries. The first person to begin unraveling the mysteries was Wolf Hirth. While on an expedition to the United States, he developed the technique of circling in a thermal to gain altitude, then gliding over a distance to gain lift from the next thermal.[2] The sport of flying unpowered aircraft began its transition from gliding to soaring.

There are, of course, variations of thermals and other forms of rising air that could be exploited for flying. In the early 1930s the German sailing enthusiasts who gathered every summer at the Wasserkuppe realized that advancing storm fronts were preceded by walls of rising air. Many of them were soon launching their aircraft into these fronts and riding them to distance records.[1] Of course, this activity was for the skilled and the brave. If the pilot did not keep his craft well positioned in the rising air, he ran the risk of being sucked into the storm, where he would have to contend with the dangers of rain, hail, darkness, and disorientation.

In May 1933, Hanna returned to Hirschberg after an unmemorable term at the medical school of Kiel University. While walking down a street in her hometown enjoying the clear spring weather, she met Wolf Hirth and his wife who were driving by. They were on their way to Grunau, where they intended to take a powered aircraft aloft to take films of the city. Hirth invited his favorite student to go to Grunau with them where she could fly the school's new glider, the Grunau-Baby. An hour later, Hanna was belted into the enclosed cockpit of the new aircraft. Because she expected only a short flight, she still wore her light summer dress and was without the benefit of helmet or goggles.

Hirth had been training Hanna to fly by instruments alone, without visual reference to views of the sky, the earth, or the horizon outside the aircraft. Hirth would use the powered aircraft to tow Hanna's glider to altitude, and she would do her banks and turns as she descended by referring to the turn-and-slip indicator and the cross-level alone. It would be an easy exercise; the air was calm and clear with only a few puffs of pure white clouds.

Hanna cast off from her tow plane when they reached an altitude of 1,200 feet. She went through her exercise and was soon about 250 feet above the ground, looking for a place to land. As she did so, she felt a quiver in the glider. She had encountered an updraft. She circled and found another, even stronger up-current. Her eyes were on her instruments as she rose at about 9 feet per second to an altitude of 1,500 feet. For the first time she looked up and saw an enormous black cloud above her. She knew that air currents rose in thermals under cumulus clouds, and she was thrilled to have the chance to fly in one. Besides, she knew how to fly by instruments; and even if she entered the bottom of the cloud, she could navigate safely. What could go wrong?

Hanna entered the darkness at the base of the cloud at 3,600 feet and was now climbing at 20 feet per second. For a brief moment she feared that the cloud, with herself in the glider, would not clear the Reisengebirge, a mountain ridge to the south of Hirschberg. But then her altitude was 5,500 feet, 300 feet higher than the highest peak of the ridge, the Schneekoppe. She was safe, she thought.

The rain and hail hit the glider with a thundering drum beat. Hanna could see the rain and hail outside the aircraft, and for a moment she began to feel fear. She was quickly through the rain and hail and still rising when the glider began to be shaken by the swirling currents of the storm. When Hanna's glider reached 9,750 feet, the instruments had been frozen by the cold, wet air. The windscreen had frosted over so that she could not see. Then the glider stalled, pitched Hanna forward against her parachute harness, and began a sickening dive in the dark.

If Hanna could not navigate by instruments she wanted to see where she was going. She smashed her fist through the mica windscreen. The wind blew through the hole soaking her in her light summer dress with the freezing rain. The glider did not seem to respond to the controls, and she released the stick. Let the plane fly itself with its own inherent stability, she thought. She would ride it as long as she could, and when the glider broke up, she would bail out. She lost track of how long the air currents tumbled her through the clouds; but, somehow, she felt warmer. And then she noticed that the gray mist outside her aircraft was becoming lighter. She was near the bottom of the cloud.

When the Grunau-Baby popped out into clear air, Hanna saw the ground above her and the cloud below: She was upside down. She quickly righted the glider and began to search for a place to land. Minutes later, Hanna guided her glider to a sliding stop on the snow beside the hotel on the Schneekoppe, the highest peak of the Riesengebirge.[3]

Hanna thought her trouble was over, but she was wrong. She called Wolf Hirth to report her location. He told her that she had landed in a neutral zone adjacent to the Czechoslovakia border where permission was required to land an aircraft. Her license to fly was in jeopardy—if she were caught.

Half an hour later, Hirth appeared in an airplane above the Schnee-koppe. He dropped a package of shock cords. Hanna had no trouble recruiting twenty men who were guests at the hotel to help her launch her glider. After a quick practice, they connected the cords to the Grunau-Baby and snapped it with its adventurous young pilot into the air for the start of her long glide into the safety of the valley below. Only after Hanna had landed, she learned that during her terrifying flight in the storm cloud, she had flown higher than anyone had flown a glider before.[4]

Wolf Hirth must have been impressed with the way Hanna handled her altitude-record setting flight into the cloud. He had taken a job as head of a new gliding school at the Hornberg, near Gmuend; and a few weeks after Hanna's flight, he offered her a job as an instructor. She was eager to take the job; and her parents, perceiving the inevitable path her life was taking, gave her permission to miss her next term at medical school.

Hanna realized that students of gliding were mostly men; and, as such, they would not be inclined to take a woman seriously as a teacher in what was then mostly a masculine pursuit. They would be even less likely to accept a twenty-two-year-old woman who was barely five feet tall as an authority and teacher. She solved the problem by giving demonstrations and involving her students in discussions, which she cleverly orchestrated to teach the principles she wanted them to learn. By the end of the course, all of her students, except one, had earned his "C" certificate.

Hanna's last student to try for the "C" certificate took off normally and flew the required pattern. He was on his final turn before landing when his glider inexplicably pitched into a steep dive. He was dead before anybody could reach the wreckage. Hanna had the unenviable chore of breaking the news to the dead man's mother. Only then did Hanna learn that the man was basically unsure of his skills as a pilot and had told others that he had dreamed he would crash during his "C" test. Even though Hanna was in no way responsible for the man's death, she was haunted by it for months to come.[5]

The patriarch of German aviation was Otto Lilienthal. He had studied the flight of birds; and in 1877 he created a device with arched wings like a bird's that glided through the air. He built more curved-wing contraptions; and in 1891 he took to the air in one while holding on to two parallel bars slung underneath the wings. Lilienthal completed over 2,000 flights with his experimental gliders before he lost his battle with gravity. In 1896 he was fatally injured when his glider crashed.[6]

Lilienthal flew gliders because his designs were not advanced enough for a motor; and, in any event, no existing motor was light and efficient enough to power an aircraft. In the 1920s and 1930s, Germans flew gliders because the Treaty of Versailles had severely restricted the use of powered aircraft by Germany. The spirit of Lilienthal reigned as the Treaty restrictions challenged the imagination of German designers to build more-efficient and more-sophisticated gliders. German pilots, mostly men who were too young to have seen action during the First World War, stretched the limits of what could be done with unpowered aircraft.

Every summer from 1920 onwards, designers and pilots met to push forward the state of the art at the Rhoen Soaring Contest held at Wasserkuppe Mountain.[7] Though the contestants were mostly Germans, the first American team participated in 1931[8] and representatives of other countries also participated, making it truly an international competition.

The Rhoen district of Germany occupies a high, grassy plateau northeast of Frankfurt am Main. Wasserkuppe Mountain rises to 950 meters, about 1,300 feet above the plain. Winds sweeping across the plateau are deflected upward by the side of the mountain, producing an ideal locale for flying a glider.[9]

The American magazine *Popular Flying* described the 1933 Rhoen Soaring Contest in a pictorial feature titled "Gliding As It Should Be: Striking Photographs of the Rhoen Mountain Gliding Contest." It wrote,

> The following figures concerning the position of gliding in Germany, where the sport is enjoyed by thousands of enthusiasts, may be of interest. During 1932, 25 new Juvenile Flying Groups were formed. The Sailing Flight Groups constructed more than 400 gliders and sailing flight machines, bringing the total number in actual daily use to 1,200; 1,214 new "B" Certificates were issued (following 913 in 1931) and 558 "C" Certificates.[10]

The photographs that accompanied the article showed dozens of young men and almost as many sleek gliders. Clearly, building and flying gliders in Germany was a popular sport, and it was growing in interest at a fast pace.

Hanna Reitsch arrived at the Wasserkuppe in the summer of 1933 with a Grunau-Baby glider and an entourage of her former flying pupils as a ground crew. The Grunau-Baby was a serviceable aircraft but no competitive match for the sleek new gliders with sculptured fuselages and stiletto-thin wings. Furthermore, Hanna was unfamiliar with the terrain and local air currents. Hanna's performance was, by her own reckoning, unremarkable. Her crew would send her aloft with the rubber shock cord, only to see her glider sink slowly to the valley below. For the two weeks of the Rhoen Contest, Hanna and her crew repeated their dismal exercise of launching, watching the Grunau-Baby sink to the base of the mountain, then hauling it to the top to try again. Hanna's depression was only deepened by the knowledge that other pilots with better aircraft and more experience were catching the wind and soaring for hours.

When the prizes for achievement were awarded on the final day, Hanna was also honored. She received several kitchen utensils that were donated by a manufacturer of kitchen equipment. She accepted these graciously, though she suspected the underlying message was that she was better suited to be in the kitchen than in an aircraft.

Whatever disappointment Hanna may have had vanished when, after the contest, Professor Walter Georgii of the *Deutsche Forschungsinstitut fur Segelflug* (German Research Institute for Glider Flight or DFS) made her an offer. Georgii was an expert, not on the design of gliders, but on the dynamics of glider flight. Apparently Georgii had been impressed by Hanna's refusal to give up in the face of failure. He was organizing an expedition to South America to study thermal conditions by means of flying gliders, and he wanted Hanna to join the group as a pilot. Georgii attached one string to his offer: Hanna would have to contribute 3,000 marks for expenses. Hanna accepted Georgii's offer, then went about raising the money.[11]

Several months earlier, after she had set the altitude record for gliders in May, Hanna had received an offer from the Ufa motion picture studio to participate in a movie about gliding. She had been asked to be a double for, and do the flying for, an actress who would portray a glider pilot. Hanna now contacted Ufa and told the film studio that her fee for the job would be 3,000 marks. The studio agreed.

Though the movie was forgettable, it gave Hanna the opportunity

to do more spectacular flying. Part of the filming was done in East
Prussia on the shores of the Baltic. Hanna flew for the cameras on
the warm summer winds above the sand dunes, staying in the air for
as long as conditions allowed. One day she was aloft for nine hours.
The following day, she stayed in the air for eleven hours and twenty
minutes. These times bested the World Endurance Record for
Women. They were not recorded as such, however, because she had
neither intended to go after the record nor set up the prescribed
conditions for recording the record beforehand.[12]

Professor Georgii's South American sailing expedition left Hamburg aboard the *Monte Pascoal* on 3 January 1934. Accompanying
Georgii were an aircraft rigger and four pilots, Hanna and three men.
A few notes about the men are in order, because they all, at different
times, figured in her story.

The most senior of the pilots was Wolf Hirth, a regular competitor
in the Rhoen Glider Contest. (It seems likely that Hirth's recom-
mendation of his protégée encouraged Georgii to invite Hanna to
join the expedition.) Hirth brought with him to South America the
Moatzagotl, a sailplane of his own design.[13]

Although only twenty-seven years old, Peter Riedel was also an old-
timer of glider flight. At the age of fifteen, he had been the youngest
competitor in the Rhoen Gliding Contests, and a regular competitor
thereafter. In 1932 he set the record for distance by flying a glider
143 miles.[14] He took a Fafnir sailplane.[13]

Heinrich Dittmar, who was known to all as "Heini," was only a
year older than Hanna.[15] He had been Peter Riedel's student in the
basics of glider flight. In his spare time during his apprenticeship at
the DFS, Dittmar built his first glider, which he gave the name "Condor." Though only twenty years old, he flew this aircraft at the 1932
Rhoen Soaring Contest and earned the first prize in the Junior class.
He brought his Condor back in 1933 and won the prize for long-
distance gliding by flying from the Wasserkuppe to Kissinger Hutte
and returning to the starting point.[15] Dittmar took his Condor on
the expedition.[13]

Hanna Reitsch, at twenty-one years of age, was the least experienced though probably the most enthusiastic member of the group.
She would fly the Grunau-Baby.[13]

When the South American sailing expedition's ship docked in Rio
de Janeiro, their careful planning collided with casual Latin attitudes.

After weeks at sea, they were anxious to unload their sailplanes and take to the sky. The people of Brazil, however, had a different agenda. They warmly welcomed their German visitors with receptions, banquets, and press conferences. Finally, after three weeks, their planes cleared customs, and they were at last free to take to the sky.

The men went aloft with their focus on altitude and distance. Hanna, being the most junior member of the team, was given duty near the airfield, where she did aerobatics in her Grunau-Baby to entertain the thousands of inhabitants of Rio de Janeiro who came out daily to watch the gliders fly. Hanna claimed that she would have preferred to participate in cross-country flights, but she also enjoyed being the center of attention.

After about four weeks in Rio de Janeiro, Professor Georgii and his expedition moved their base to Sao Paulo, which lies about 280 miles to the west. There Hanna finally got her chance to fly with the men in their quest for altitude and distance. One of the reasons for going to South America was to explore the thermals, which were rare in Germany but common on the plains of South America. Peter Riedel and Heini Dittmar had already reached a cloud base about 6,500 feet above when Hanna was towed into the sky by a powered airplane. Although she was still at a relatively low altitude, Hanna thought she was already in the grip of a thermal, and she cast off her tow rope. She found to her dismay that her aircraft kept sinking back toward the town. Hanna was learning the hard way the complexity of thermals. A thermal is commonly caused by the warm ground, heated by the sun, transferring its heat to the air, which then rises in a broad column. Under certain conditions, however, the air may rise, not like a column, but as a bubble would rise in a glass of beer. The air below the bubble offered a glider pilot no lift, and it was in that dismal spot under the bubble where Hanna found herself.

Hanna searched for a landing site among the rooftops and saw only one within reach. It was, she realized to her horror, a soccer field with a game in progress, surrounded by a crowd of enthusiastic fans. The players dove for the ground and scattered as she swooped across a goal and came to a stop. The crowd went wild over the stunning interruption of the game. Fortunately nobody was injured, and Hanna was again a celebrity, finding good will where there might have been a bloody disaster.

From Brazil, the expedition went southwest to Buenos Aires and then the pampas of Argentina. These grassy plains gave birth to thermals far more powerful than any of the group had experienced in Germany. The thermals were what the pilots of the expedition wanted and needed if they were to soar high and far and, in the process, set records. Their guides in finding the thermals were the native vultures, or "urubus," as they were called by the native peoples. The birds earned their keep in the ecology of the South American plains by cleaning up carrion. They were black, about the size of geese, and as ugly as death. American western movies would have one believe that flocks of vultures circle overhead waiting for something they see on the ground below to die. In reality, vultures catch the lift of the thermals as an energy-efficient form of travel. The vultures of the Argentine pampas circled in groups of hundreds, neatly indicating the positions of the thermals; and they accepted the larger creatures guided by humans who wanted to soar among them.[16]

The members of the South American glider expedition had their greatest successes in Argentina. Wolf Hirth performed an aerobatic tour de force when he did sixty-seven successive loops in his glider. This was, at the time, a new world record. Heini Dittmar recklessly allowed himself to get sucked into a storm cloud and be pushed toward its top. Although it was a terrifying experience for him, he set a new altitude record for gliders. Peter Riedel covered a distance of ninety-three miles by flying from thermal to thermal in his plane; and, in the process, he set a new soaring record for distance. On the same day Riedel set his distance record, Hanna Reitsch was able to make a flight that lasted some two and a half to three hours. Hanna's flight was for her a significant achievement because it earned for her the Silver Soaring Medal.[17] (Today it is known as the Silver Badge, and its award is sanctioned by the *Federation Aeronautique International* for a cross-country flight of at least thirty-one miles [fifty kilometers].)[18] She was the twenty-fifth pilot and first woman to earn this award.[17]

The expedition to South America gave Hanna not only success in flying but also an education about men. On the long shipboard journey to Brazil, Heini Dittmar attempted to court his attractive young colleague. Hanna, whose obsession was flying, not men, found Dittmar a nuisance and declined his advances. However, a few days before returning to Germany, Hanna met a young Spanish pilot she took more seriously. In a moment of comraderie, Hanna clasped his hand and was surprised when he took her gesture as an invitation to romance. Hanna was, she realized, attracted to the man; yet her puritanical upbringing held her in check. In her confused attempt to escape, she told her suitor that she had, alas, a fiancé. She soon regretted her lie and sent him a letter of apology in the hope of retrieving the magic moment. He did not reply, and Hanna set sail for home on 13 April 1934, wiser, if not happier, for the experience.[19]

The year that passed from the spring of 1933, when Hanna Reitsch ended her second term of medical school, to the spring of 1934, when she returned from South America, was the first year of Nazi power. Great changes had taken place in Germany and in German aviation. The Reich Air Ministry was the governmental body that was in charge of civil aviation in post–World War I Germany. When Adolf Hitler became Germany's Chancellor in March 1933, he appointed Hermann Goering, his second in command in the Nazi party, to the position of Minister of Aviation. Under Goering's leadership and with Hitler's repudiation of the Treaty of Versailles, the Air Ministry consolidated the paramilitary activities that would result in the formal formation of the Luftwaffe only two years later. The Reich Air Ministry began to pour its support into aircraft development. Through the League of Air Sports, it began to train military pilots.[20]

The DFS also fared well under the Nazi regime. It had begun at the Wasserkuppe in 1925 as the Rhoen-Rositten-Gesselschaft, an organization dedicated to research into motorless flight. In the autumn of 1933,[21] it moved to Darmstadt-Greischeim where it could use an airfield and tow planes not available at the Wasserkuppe.[22] When it arrived at its new location, the Rhoen-Rositten-Gesselschaft changed its name to *Deutsche Forschungsinstitut fur Segelflug*, or DFS. Because the DFS was a government-supported institute, it received its share of the new regime's money. The DFS became a rapidly growing organization with a need for skilled glider pilots.

Professor Walter Georgii, director of the DFS,[21,22] was short on pilots and impressed by Hanna Reitsch's enthusiasm and growing skill. In the spring of 1934, on the return voyage of his South American sailing expedition, he offered a position with the DFS to Hanna despite her rough edges and occasional misadventures. Hanna took the job without a second thought. She reported for duty in June 1934.[22]

With her acceptance of Georgii's offer to join the DFS, Hanna effectively gave up her medical education, which she had been shamefully neglecting in any case. She abandoned her childhood dream of being a flying missionary doctor. The poor little black children would have to get well and find salvation without her. Hanna never recorded what her father thought about her abandoning the medical studies he had subsidized.

Heini Dittmar had been hanging around the Rhoen-Rositten-Gesselschaft, the predecessor of the DFS, since 1929, as an unpaid assistant to Alexander Lippisch. Lippisch was a highly imaginative aircraft designer who, in 1928, was first to attach a rocket propulsion unit to an aircraft.[23] By the 1930s, Lippisch had turned his attention to designing and building radical delta-winged, tailless gliders and powered aircraft.[21] After Dittmar returned from South America, Lippisch offered him the position as his primary test pilot. Dittmar eagerly accepted and also went to work at the DFS in 1934.[24]

Hanna's first two years with the DFS gave her the opportunities to gain practical experience in research flying; to continue competing in glider competitions; to get advanced pilot training not generally available, especially to a woman; and to participate in foreign flying projects, thereby letting her gain more international recognition.

These are some of the projects she took on:

Initially, Hanna was assigned flights to make meteorological measurements, to traverse long distances, and to attain high altitude. These paid off for Hanna with the Women's World Record for distance of over 100 miles (accomplished while off duty) and the Women's World Altitude record of 2,800 meters.[22,25]

In September 1934, at the invitation of the Finnish government, she participated in a program in which German glider pilots gave instructions to student pilots in Finland.[26]

After the expedition to Finland, Hanna requested from the Reich Air Ministry permission to attend the Civil Airways Training School in Stettin. The school was run in paramilitary fashion, which is not surprising because the Reich Air Ministry was clandestinely training future Luftwaffe pilots. Hanna received permission to attend the school, where she gained experience with twin-engine powered aircraft.[27]

After her return to the DFS at Darmstadt, Hanna conducted meteorological research flights at night in a powered aircraft.[28]

In May 1935 Hanna was part of a team of pilots who went to Lisbon, Portugal, to give glider demonstrations at the "Festivas Lisboa." By this time, Hermann Goering had revealed that Germany had created an air force, the Luftwaffe, which was specifically denied it by the Treaty of Versailles.[29] Furthermore, Germany had instituted general peacetime conscription. These events created international tensions, and they complicated Hanna's transit through France to Portugal for the festival. Hanna charmed and bulled her way through, but her travails were a portent of the greater tensions that would soon take Europe into their grip.[30]

By 1935 the DFS had grown to the extent that it was divided into departments. Hanna went to work as a test pilot for the department headed by Hans Jacobs, a glider designer. Jacobs had gone to work for Alexander Lippisch as his assistant at the Rhoen-Rositten-Gesellschaft in 1927.[21] With the move to Darmstadt, the name change to the DFS, and the expansion under the new political regime in 1933, Jacobs became an independent designer, gaining his own department in 1935. Although Jacobs' gliders were incremental modifications of conventional designs, he was very successful; and he soon began to overshadow his mentor, Lippisch, at the DFS.[31] Lippisch's pilot, Heini Dittmar, also found himself uncomfortably in the shadow of Jacobs' pilot, Hanna Reitsch.

As part of becoming a test pilot, Hanna had to fill some woeful gaps in her education. Though she had shown exceptional skill at flying aircraft, especially gliders, she knew nothing about their construction. She was also ignorant of the systematic testing of new aircraft and the incrementally increasing demands placed on it by a test pilot to tease out its weaknesses. Hanna began her remedial education by haunting the glider construction shop at the DFS and seeing, in all its details, the construction of the new sailplane designed by Hans Jacobs, the Crane.

Hanna's flight testing of the Crane began cautiously with a tow behind a tow plane that carried her no more than 20 feet above the ground. When she was satisfied that the aircraft was stable, she had the tow plane carry the Crane to an altitude of 6,500 feet. She cast off the tow rope and took it through a series of exercises to determine its flight characteristics. When she landed, she gave her test results and impressions to Jacobs and his crew, who then went about modifying the craft. After a series of test flights followed by engineering improvements, the Crane was deemed airworthy; and Hanna went on to other projects.[32]

In the summer of 1935 Hanna began testing Hans Jacobs' Sea Eagle, a glider with an outwardly conventional appearance but with a design intended to permit it to take off from and land on water. In the initial tests, while being towed behind an amphibious flying boat, Hanna was able to lift the Sea Eagle into the air. However, the weight of several hundred feet of waterlogged tow rope dragged the airplane back into the water, and it completely submerged before popping back to the surface undamaged. This mishap had proven the strength of the aircraft's design, but it also demonstrated the need for a modified takeoff procedure and a floating tow line. With these improvements in place, Hanna brought the test flights of the Sea Eagle to a successful conclusion.[33]

Hanna's next project also involved taking off from the water, but she tested the launching method rather than the aircraft. A winch that would spool-up a cable with increasing speed had been used previously for land-based glider launches. One such device was set up on the shore of a lake. The plan was to haul in the Sea Eagle with Hanna at its control, like a fisherman on shore would reel in a catch. At the optimal moment, Hanna was to lift the aircraft off the water and drop the tow line, then circle back to land in the water. The trick would be to get safely airborne without ramming the glider into the winch on the shore. Hanna successfully completed the tests, but the launching method seems to have been dropped because of its potential for disaster.[34]

In 1936 two men who would have a profound influence on her career and life entered Hanna's life. The first of these was Ernst Udet, possibly the most famous and respected pilot in Germany. In the First World War, Udet had shot down sixty-two enemy aircraft, second in victories only to Manfred von Richthofen, the legendary "Red Baron." After Germany's first defeat, Udet made a living as an aircraft designer and a stunt flier. When the Luftwaffe was created in 1935, he joined with the rank of General Major, and he became Chief of the Technical Office of the Reich Air Ministry the following year. In 1939 Udet assumed the position of Inspector-General of the Luftwaffe with responsibility for aircraft and weapons procurement. Udet was a showman with a great enthusiasm for all things relating to flight. He had cosmopolitan tastes; and he was known for his affinity for liquor, cigars, and beautiful women.[35,36]

Udet made his first flight in a glider in 1934 or 1935 and became an instant devotee of the sport. "Sail flying is, after all," he commented after his first glider flight, "the only genuine flying, and the highest type of aeronautics."[7] It is probable that Ernst Udet and

Hanna Reitsch first met because of their shared interest in glider flight. They both participated in demonstrations of glider flights at the winter Olympic games at Garmisch in early 1936 and the summer games in Berlin that same year.[37] Hanna often visited Udet at his Berlin apartment, as did practically everybody else who was of consequence in German aviation. Those who saw them together—at least in the years before the war—felt that their entire relationship revolved around their mutual interest in aviation.[38]

General Robert Ritter von Greim was nearly the match of Ernst Udet as a pilot and as a force within the Luftwaffe. He finished the First World War with the downing of twenty-eight enemy planes to his credit.[39] Like Udet, he had been awarded the *Pour le Merite*, the "Blue Max," Germany's highest award for valor. He had also been knighted, earning the right to add "Ritter von" (Knight of) to his name;[40] but friend and foe alike still called him simply "Greim." After the war, Greim and Udet had, for a brief time, made a living by flying against each other in exhibition dogfights.[41] Greim then studied law at the University of Munich. There, he made the acquaintance of Adolph Hitler and, in 1920, took the future Fuehrer on his first airplane flight. Greim had piloted them from Munich toward Berlin where Hitler hoped to capitalize on a right-wing coup attempt that was in progress. Greim was forced to land short of their destination; and Hitler, apparently shaken by the experience, put off his second flight for many years. Greim was one of the first to answer Goering's call to join the newly created Luftwaffe. When its existence was made public in 1935, Goering named Greim First Squadron Leader of the Luftwaffe.[39]

At forty-four, Greim was famous, self-assured, and rapidly rising in the new service.[39] Like Ernst Udet, Greim was impressed by the gutsy little pilot who was twenty years his junior. Though Udet would introduce Hanna to the aviation establishment, Greim would eventually become the central figure in her life. Between Reitsch and Greim flared the tiniest spark that would smolder into the flames of romance and doom.

Ernst Udet and Robert Ritter von Greim had the opportunity of watching Hanna perform as a test pilot at Darmstadt-Griesheim in 1936.

Because of their light weight, gliders were particularly delicate aircraft. When put under stress—for example by flying through turbulent air or diving at high speed—they risked breaking up. To control the fragile aircraft when their speed was about to get out of control, Hans Jacobs had devised self-operating dive brakes. The brakes were perforated panels that would automatically lift up over each wing placing their flat side toward the air flow when the glider's speed became too great for safety. Powered aircraft, especially high-performance aircraft such as fighters and dive bombers, also experienced the stresses of high-speed flight, and like the glider, they risked disastrous structural failure. Hanna had tested Jacobs' dive brakes during their development, and she was given the responsibility of demonstrating them to a group of Luftwaffe generals including Udet and Greim at Darmstadt-Griesheim.

High above the airfield, Hanna put the glider into a dive, leaving altitude soundlessly behind. As the tiny aircraft's speed increased, the dive brakes popped into place. The glider fell for over 10,000 feet. Its speed was held rigidly in check at 125 miles per hour by brakes. Then, just 600 feet above the airfield, Hanna pulled the glider out of its dive, closed the dive brakes, and landed.

Udet was sufficiently impressed by Hanna's demonstration of Hans Jacobs' dive brakes to later arrange for her to give another demonstration of the self-operating dive brakes before the designers of Germany's aircraft manufacturers in the spring of 1937.[42] Thereafter, Udet became Hanna's mentor within the German aviation establishment.

The Luftwaffe was comprised of groups of trained pilots with a large number of untested aircraft. In late July 1936 Francisco Franco, who led a revolt of the Spanish military against its constitutional republican monarchy, offered Germany a testing ground. Franco asked for military aid from his fellow European fascist leaders, Mussolini of Italy and Hitler. Although Germany had no national interest in the Spanish civil war, Hitler was eager to lend a hand. He supported creation of a new fascist state south of France, which would help occupy the political energies of both France and Great Britain. Also, Mussolini, who was inclined to aid Franco, would be further pressured into doing so, thereby undercutting any rapprochement between Italy and France or Great Britain. Germany sent technicians, tanks, planes, and the Luftwaffe's Condor Legion to Franco. In April 1937 this group distinguished itself in the world's consciousness by destroying the Basque town of Guernica and a good many of its civilian inhabitants.[43] Spain had been the test by fire of the Luftwaffe's pilots and its aircraft. Guernica had been the testing ground of its dive bombers, which, of course, had dive brakes.

The German press, quite understandably, neglected to report the exploits of the Condor Legion over Guernica; but it proudly praised the achievements of its civilian sport pilots. In May 1937 Hanna Reitsch was one of a group of five pilots who made the first glider flights over the Alps from Salzburg, Austria, to Pieve di Cadore in Italy. It was a triumph of altitude (13,000 feet) and distance (over 100 miles). Hanna's achievement put her in the German headlines.[44]

Chapter 3

The Iron Cross

By the summer of 1937, Hans Jacobs and his team had finished fine-tuning the dive brakes, and Hanna had finished testing them. With this successful completion of the program came recognition for Hanna. Ernst Udet arranged for her to receive the honorary title of *Flugkapitan*, or "Flight Capitain," in recognition of her contributions to aeronautical research. Until then, only pilots of Lufthansa, the German civil airline, had been eligible for this title.[1,2] Other test pilots, including Heini Dittmar, would later eventually receive it; but Hanna set the new standard. The ceremony at which she received the title was noteworthy in that it marked her first meeting with Adolf Hitler.

Hanna's rank of *Flugkapitan* gave her the credentials—if not credibility—she needed for her next assignment. General Udet gave her a job as a test pilot at the Luftwaffe's aircraft testing station at Rechlin.

Hanna's initial reception at Rechlin was warm—or so she thought, but as the days passed, and as she flew higher into the world of the test pilots, she began to believe that there was a chill in the air over

Rechlin. In male-dominated Nazi Germany, Hanna had invaded the realm of the manliest of pursuits. She had hurdled the razor's edge of safety and was flight testing the Nazi war machine's hottest new weapons. Somehow she had gained the favor of General Udet; and there she was, in the place of a man, taking a precious slice of the danger and the glory.

Hanna stayed at Rechlin because she loved flying; because her mentor, Ernst Udet, had sent her there; because she was loyal to her country and its Nazi leadership; and because she was stubborn. She got into the cockpits of Stukas, fighters, and bombers. She flew everything with a propeller and wings, and she loved every minute she was off the ground.

When Hanna's first tour of duty at Rechlin as a test pilot for the Luftwaffe came to an end, she could not point to any single act of hers that benefited the Luftwaffe, but the experience certainly added to her credentials as a test pilot. She returned to duty with the DFS at Darmstadt; but, with Germany's entry into war, she would be called upon again to test its newest, most radical aircraft.[2]

One of Hanna's most challenging yet most successful enterprises after becoming Udet's protégée and a test pilot for the Luftwaffe was the public demonstration of the first truly successful helicopter. The aircraft, called a *Hubschrauber* in German, was the Focke-Achgelis FW 61, which was designed by Gerd Achgelis and built under the direction of Professor Heinrich Focke of Bremen in 1937.

The FW 61's solution to flight without wings, although unlike anything we now consider a helicopter, was elegant in its simple design. The aircraft had at its core a conventional airplane fuselage with an open cockpit and a tricycle landing gear. The wings were replaced with two outrigger booms to which were mounted two large vertically directed propellers. The propellers were driven by a motor housed in the nose of the aircraft. The pilot controlled the helicopter by adjusting the throttle, which varied the speed of the engine and the lift, and by adjusting the pitch of the propellers forward or backward, to the left or to the right.[3]

Though its design may have been conceptually simple, flying the FW 61 helicopter challenged a pilot's normal instincts. It called upon a pilot's sense of balance as a substitute for his—or her—sense of forward motion for stability. If flying a conventional aircraft was like riding a bicycle, flying the helicopter was like riding a unicycle.

The assignment to test-fly the FW 61 helicopter for the Luftwaffe was given initially to a man named Karl Franke from Rechlin. Franke invited Hanna Reitsch to join him on the flight to Bremen where he would fly the new aircraft. When they arrived, Professor Focke assumed that Hanna was also to fly the helicopter, and Franke graciously let him keep this misconception.[3] Franke began his first flight, and when he had disposed of a ground tether intended to give him a sense of safety, he enjoyed a half-hour flight. Franke then turned the controls of the helicopter over to Hanna Reitsch.[4]

Hanna understood that her instincts and all the old rules of flying had to be discarded; and for that reason, she was able to control the helicopter whereas others might lose their nerve. With practice she was soon able to do an aerial ballet with the helicopter. A few weeks after she first saw the helicopter, she demonstrated it before Charles Lindbergh, who was in self-imposed exile in Germany. According to Hanna, Lindbergh called Focke's helicopter "the most striking aeronautical development he had ever seen."[5]

Ernst Udet was no less impressed by the radical new aircraft and by Hanna's achievement in flying it. He had, however, a conventional attitude toward flight that required wings and forward motion. He had no interest in trying to fly the helicopter himself and apparently saw limited use for it in the Luftwaffe; yet he considered the possibility that it might impress the Army. Udet arranged for Hanna to demonstrate the helicopter to the Chief of the Army General Staff and a group of high-ranking Army and Luftwaffe officers. For a conventional counterpoint, Udet would demonstrate the new Fieseler *Storch*, a single-engine, high-wing light plane with short takeoff and landing capability.

The day of the demonstration arrived with a thick fog and visibility of less than fifty yards. Udet and Reitsch were undeterred. Udet took off in the Fieseler *Storch*; and thereafter, the exceptional performance characteristics of the light plane—whatever they might have been— were hidden by the fog. Hanna and the helicopter were less affected by the weather. She guided her craft forward, backward, side to side, in various patterns, and was able to stay within view of the Army contingent. When she landed, they gave her a round of applause. The Luftwaffe gave her the Military flying medal for her achievements with the helicopter and other aircraft. She was the first woman to receive it.

Hanna's performance in the Focke-Achgelis FW 61 may have been a hit with the Generals of the Luftwaffe and German Army, but foreign newspapers received the story of the helicopter's performance with skepticism. Udet felt obligated to see that Germany received credit for the first practical helicopter, so he arranged for his protégée, Hanna Reitsch, to demonstrate the revolutionary aircraft at the International Automobile Exhibition to be held in Berlin's Deutschlandhalle, an indoor stadium, in February 1938.[5] The posters advertising Hanna's demonstration of the helicopter appalled her.

KISUAHEIL!

Deutschlandhalle
—Kisuaheil—
Through the tropics at 200 Miles per Hour

Dancing Girls, Fakirs, Clowns, Blackamoors, and
Hanna Reitsch Will Fly the Helicopter

Not only was Hanna to be part of a circus, she was at the bottom of the bill. She was concerned that her participation in a frivolous entertainment would undercut her efforts to be taken seriously as a professional pilot.

The program at the International Automobile Exposition had little to do with automobiles. It was about—mostly—the African colonies Germany had lost at the end of the First World War, and its desire to see its days of glory as a colonial power returned. The body of the program consisted of variety and circus acts performed on the floor of the Deutschlandhalle, and it concluded with Hanna's demonstration.

In the beams of spotlights, the silver helicopter with a swastika on its tail and "Deutschland" lettered on its fuselage was rolled into the arena. Hanna pushed the throttle forward, and as the helicopter rose beneath the roof of the stadium, the members of the audience held their hats and programs tightly to keep them from being blown away. Hanna took the helicopter through her program of flight within the limited confines of the enclosed stadium, gliding forward, backward, and sideways. She concluded her performance by giving a stiff-armed Nazi salute, then returned to the floor of the Deutschlandhalle. To her surprise, when she had landed, the spectators were polite in their applause but disappointed in the overall performance. After all, they had been promised "through the tropics at 200 miles per hour," and the helicopter had merely flown a precision course at a very slow speed.

Hanna flew the helicopter at every performance during the three weeks of the Exposition, and she found it a bizarre experience. One circus performer, a high-wire-artist, appreciated her act and accepted her as a colleague. As the days and performances passed, though, the spectators and the German public began to understand the technical achievement of the helicopter and of Hanna's demonstration. And contrary to her fears, the helicopter and her indoor flight drew an enthusiastic response from the aeronautical world.[6]

In the years from 1937 to 1939, Hanna scored many successes in gliding competitions, setting several distance records in the process. She began in late 1937 by flying from the Wasserkuppe in central Germany to Hamburg in the north, thereby setting the world's long-distance soaring record. Hanna followed that success in 1938 with a flight from Darmstadt to Wasserkuppe and back, a round trip of about 140 miles. That same year, she flew from the Frisian Islands, on the edge of the North Sea, to Breslau in Silesia, crossing most of the width of Germany. Then in July of 1939, she earned another record by gliding from Magdeburg, in central Germany, to Stettin, near the shores of the Baltic Sea.[7]

Understandably, these successes in Hanna's career diverted her attention from events taking place in Germany that would profoundly affect the world, her homeland, and her own life. On 12 March 1938 the independent government of Austria succumbed to Nazi subversion from within and bullying by Hitler and the German government from without. It submitted to the *Anschluss*, annexation by Germany.[8] On 30 September 1938 Neville Chamberlain, Prime Minister of Great Britain announced that he, Hitler, and other European leaders had agreed to the cession of the Sudetenland from Czechoslovakia to Germany.[9] Hanna was in the United States at the time to demonstrate aerobatics in a glider at the International Air Races in Cleveland. She regretted that she and her group were recalled to Germany "amid disturbing news from Czechoslovakia."[10]

If Hanna and any other good Germans had failed to understand the Nazi regime's attitude toward the Jews, it was made brutally public during the night of 9–10 November 1938, *Krystalnacht*. Nazi thugs roamed the streets of Germany beating Jews, destroying their shops and businesses, and burning synagogues. The shattered glass on the

streets gave the event its terrifyingly beautiful name of crystal night.
The Holocaust had officially begun.[11] The pretense that the Nazis
wanted only a unified Germany and peace was discarded on 1 September 1939 when German forces invaded Poland.[12] The Second
World War had begun, and it was time to live one's allegiance. From
here on until long after the destruction of the Third Reich, Hanna
gave up the joy of flying freely with the birds and of following the
winds in the sky.

Hanna Reitsch counted herself a good German and went to work
for the great patriotic cause of the Fatherland. She continued to test-
fly gliders designed by Hans Jacobs at the DFS, but these new designs
had military purposes. The more notable of her projects are discussed
next.

Soon after completion of the work on dive brakes, Jacobs' group
began work on a transport glider. In her biography, Hanna claimed
that the initial concept had a benign purpose, the delivery of mail.
Any advantage the transport glider had over a powered aircraft was
minimal, however, because it still needed the tow plane to return it
to the air so that it could be reused. With the advent of war, the
cargo of the glider became ten armed men, and the design of the
aircraft evolved into the DFS-230 troop-carrying glider. The glider
was towed into the air behind a Junkers 52. Hanna piloted it for test
flights and later demonstrations for the military brass: Luftwaffe Generals Udet and Greim and Field Marshals Kesselring, Model, and
Milch. Her demonstration flights generated great enthusiasm for the
aircraft in the military leadership and further solidified her standing
with the senior military men of the Third Reich.[13,14]

When the invasion of France was postponed from November 1939
until February 1940, Hanna tested landing brakes for the DFS-230,
which would increase the safety and accuracy of landing.[15] The troop-
carrying glider was eventually used to great effect in the invasions of
Belgium in 1940.[16,17]

After her success with the ten-passenger DFS-230, Hanna found
herself testing a series of aircraft and systems that had serious, and,
in some cases, lethal design flaws. The first of these aircraft was the
Messerschmitt 321 *Gigant*. Two hundred of these aircraft were to be
used in Operation Sea Lion, Germany's invasion of England, which
was planned for 1940.[16,18]

The *Gigant*, "Giant" in English, was a high-wing monoplane glider
of unprecedented dimensions. It had a wingspan of over 180 feet and

a length of over 92 feet. Its empty weight was 26,460 pounds; and it could carry over 24 tons, giving it a loaded weight of 74,970 pounds. It could carry 22 tons of freight, a small tracked vehicle, or a company of soldiers. The *Gigant*'s flight characteristics were reported to have been graceful despite its cumbersome controls. It made smooth, graceful landings like single-occupant sports gliders.[19]

The *Gigant*'s problem, as Hanna discovered, was getting off the ground. The huge glider was towed behind a four-engine Junkers 290, and its takeoff was assisted by four rocket units that were attached to its wings. Hanna found the performance of the tow plane and the *Gigant* discouraging. When they tried again, they replaced the single tow-plane with what was called the *Troika-Schlepp*, three twin-engine Messerschmitt Bf 110s. Even with the rocket assists on the glider, the tow planes were close to stalling at takeoff. When, on one test flight, one of the tow planes stalled and the takeoff had to be aborted, Hanna refused to participate in further tests. The *Gigant* was, in her mind, too dangerous.

In a test flight soon after, the rockets on one side of the *Gigant* failed to fire. The *Troika-Schlepp* and *Gigant* assembly was thrown out of balance with disastrous consequences: The three pilots of the tow planes, the six-man crew of the *Gigant*, and 110 troops on the glider— a total of 119 men—were killed.[16,18]

The Messerschmitt 321 *Gigant* eventually entered service in May 1941, after the Luftwaffe had lost the Battle of Britain and the invasion of Britain had been postponed indefinitely. It had an undistinguished career ferrying freight to the eastern front.[19]

Another ill-conceived aircraft Hanna Reitsch tested was a glider intended for use as a flying gasoline tanker. The mother plane would tow it behind until it needed fuel; then it would fill up from the glider. Because the glider was intended to not have a pilot, its critical specification was that it have inherent stability, that it return to a level course even if it was thrown upside-down by air turbulence.

A prototype with controls for a very small pilot was built. Hanna took the flying gasoline tanker aloft—under tow, of course—and put it into dangerous maneuvers to see if it would right itself. The results for Hanna were violent attacks of airsickness and a justifiable fear of a fatal end to her flights. The flying gasoline tanker proved to be impracticable, and its development was discontinued.[20]

Hanna then went on to test a method that would allow a small observation plane that had taken off from the deck of a warship to

land in a short deck space on its return. The shipboard landing strip
was to be constructed of a series of parallel ropes about a hundred
feet long and three feet apart that were stretched in a ramp that rose
about twenty feet to the top of a barrier at its far end. The pilot
would use the parallel ropes as a landing strip and be stopped by a
number of braking devices attached to the ropes.

A rope landing structure was built at an airfield for Hanna's tests;
and because no suitable powered aircraft was yet available, she chose
to use a glider for her test landings. On the first landing, a gust of
wind tipped the glider at the last moment and pitched the cockpit
under a rope. Had Hanna not ducked, she would have been decapi-
tated. The second landing went exactly as planned but ended with
the nose of the plane uncomfortably close to the barrier at the far
end of the ropes. On Hanna's third landing, her glider went over the
end of the landing structure; but, fortunately, it hung by its tail.
Hanna's rescuers reached her by fire ladder. The project was wisely
abandoned.[21]

As Hanna Reitsch explained it, her test flying for the Luftwaffe was
often for the purpose of saving lives, German lives.[22] During the Battle of Britain, many Luftwaffe planes and their crews were lost, not
to the heroic flying of RAF pilots, but to chance encounters with
barrage balloons. The gas-filled leviathans floated over the English
countryside connected to earth only by steel cables. The cables were
difficult to see under the best daylight flying conditions, and they
were an invisible peril to Luftwaffe pilots on night raids. An aircraft
flying 200 miles per hour or faster would meet one of these wires,
and a wing would be sliced off, tumbling the plane out of the sky
without its crew ever knowing what evil beast had sent them to their
deaths.

Hans Jacobs devised a system that would defeat the barrage balloons. He installed fenders to protect the engines and wings and to
divert the cables to the wing tips, where a simple device would cut
the cable. Hanna, who would conduct the flight tests, reasoning that
at the moment of impact, bits of cable and wing might come slashing
through the cockpit, wanted to be some place less vulnerable and
nearer the escape hatch in the event that something went wrong.
After becoming airborne, she would turn control over to her copilot
and move to the rear gun turret where a duplicate set of controls had

been installed. When she was at the second set of controls, the copilot would join her at the rear of the plane.

Hanna conducted the initial tests of Hans Jacobs' cable cutter at Rechlin. She guided her plane through cables held aloft by balloons that started at 2.7 millimeters in diameter and increased in thickness to the ultimate diameter of 8.9 millimeters. She went through most of the testing sequence, but was forced to stop before completion by headaches and high fever. She had contracted scarlet fever and was hospitalized.[23]

Hanna languished in the hospital for months without the aid of effective antibiotics while the disease ravaged her body. It affected her eyes, necessitating that her room be kept in total darkness. She developed muscular rheumatism, and the infection also affected her heart.

During Hanna's convalescence, another pilot completed the tests of Jacobs' cable cutter. Most of the Luftwaffe brass was skeptical of the value of the cable cutter; but one senior officer, Robert Ritter von Greim, took it into battle. Hanna reported that Greim's men wrote to her with thanks when the device showed its worth. Regrettably for the Third Reich, Jacobs' device was too heavy to have general utility.[24]

After a three-month absence from the Luftwaffe, Hanna returned to duty to find that there was still work to do on cable cutters; but there were also changes in the program. First, a cable-cutting device of a new design was ready to be tested. It was, simply, a strip of razor-sharp steel fastened to the leading edge of the wing. Also, testing of the cable cutters had been transferred from the aircraft testing facility at Rechlin to the balloon testing site at Saarow, where it was easier to manage the targets. Once again, Hanna's job was to demonstrate that in a midair encounter, the cable would part before the modified wing.

Hanna and the Luftwaffe crew had worked for weeks testing the new, light, balloon cutter, working their way up through thicker and tougher cables. Now, Hanna was to cut through a cable that had been carried from England over to the continent by a loose barrage balloon. It was 5.6 millimeters in diameter and composed of only five or six steel strands.

Hanna was in the cockpit of the Dornier 17 assessing her target. Because only a short length of the cable from England was available, the balloon it anchored was uncomfortably close to the ground, float-

ing not much higher than the treetops. Furthermore, the broad side
of the balloon had a tendency to catch the wind like a sail and drag
the cable off at an angle. From her position aloft, Hanna thought that
the low altitude and steeply slanting cable made the test dangerous,
but the ground crew gave her an "all clear" signal. Hanna moved to
the controls in the rear gun turret and began her approach.

Unknown to Hanna, Ernst Udet had stopped over on his way to a
conference with Hitler. Udet decided to stay to watch his old friend
and protégée fly through the cable that anchored the barrage balloon.
The ground crew should have postponed the test because of the
windy and dangerous conditions, but nobody wanted to disappoint
the General.

Hanna guided the Dornier 17 just above treetop level—too low to
bail out if anything went wrong—and aligned the starboard (right)
wing to intersect the imaginary line in the sky where the cable should
be.

WHAM.

The cable parted and chunks of a metal propeller blade shot
through the cockpit. The starboard engine, lacking the resistance of
an intact airscrew, began to race. Hanna swiftly turned off the engine
before it could tear itself loose from the wing and leave her in an
even more perilous situation.

From the ground, General Udet had seen the low-flying bomber
slash into the balloon cable; then he watched in horror as metal frag-
ments filled the air around the point of impact. The aircraft, making
clear sounds of distress, disappeared over the treetops. Udet and the
ground crew waited for the inevitable sounds of tearing metal and
exploding fuel.

Hanna limped the crippled bomber to an airfield several miles away
and brought it to a safe landing. Udet followed her there in his own
plane. When they met on the ground, he was paler that she had ever
seen him, and he was so shaken, he was unable to speak. When Udet
regained his composure, he continued on to his meeting with Hitler.
He told the Fuehrer every terrifying detail about Hanna's near fatal
test flight.[25]

On 27 March 1941 Hanna Reitsch was entertained by Reich Marshal and Commander in Chief of the Luftwaffe Hermann Goering at
his palatial residence in Berlin. In recognition of her bravery in service to the Luftwaffe, he presented her with a special version of the

Gold Medal for Military Flying. Goering's appreciation was accented by the ring of diamonds that encircled the golden eagle with outstretched wings.[26]

The following day, 28 March 1941, Hanna received an even greater honor. At the Reich Chancellery, Hitler conferred on her the Iron Cross, Second Class. Hanna Reitsch was only the second woman in the history of Germany to receive the award. She wore both awards proudly over the left breast of her tunic.[26] Hanna Reitsch had become the darling of the leaders of Nazi Germany and an ironic model of German womanhood in a country where the primary roles for women were to tend to domestic affairs and breed more true Aryans.[27]

On 4 April 1941 Hanna Reitsch was given a heroine's reception in her hometown of Hirschberg in Silesia. The mayor personally brought Hanna by car to Hirschberg, where she was greeted at the city limits by students from her alma mater, the Grunau Gliding School, and by the local Luftwaffe detachment. The car passed crowds of cheering citizens and singing children, through a sea of flowers and flags. When they arrived at the Town Hall, Hanna was presented with the Scroll of Honorary Citizenship, the city's highest honorary award. Hanna was then taken to the school she had attended as a child. There, the people of Grunau presented her with a Grunau-Baby sailplane. The day of her triumphant return to her Hirschberg home was, possibly, the last truly happy day of her life.[28]

A tragic postscript to this part of Hanna Reitsch's story is the death of her mentor, Ernst Udet, less than a year later. On 17 November 1941, while at his Berlin apartment, Udet put a bullet through his head.[29,30]

To avoid scandal, Goering insisted it be reported that Udet had died accidentally while testing a new air weapon. Udet was given a state funeral on 21 November. Goering walked behind his coffin on the way to the cemetery and gave a tearful eulogy for his lost comrade. When Goering finished, he stood beside Hitler while a band played the funeral march from *Gotterdammerung*.[31]

Inevitably, reports of Udet's suicide leaked out. He had been under suspicion of having aided Rudolf Hess in his flight to Britain in May 1941. The Luftwaffe's failures in the Battle of Britain and on the eastern front with equipment he had procured were a heavy weight. Finally, Udet had a violent argument with Goering, in which the Reich Marshal had tried to force Udet to accept an unfair share of the responsibility for the Luftwaffe's failures. Common speculation held that Udet had been depressed.[29,31]

Udet's Luftwaffe colleague General Bernd von Brauchitsch offered a different opinion. Udet, he said, had taken his life because he found himself overwhelmed by his bureaucratic responsibilities for the Luftwaffe—for which he had little aptitude and interest—and because of trouble with a woman. Von Brauchitsch did not identify the woman.[32] Hanna Reitsch made no mention of the death of Ernst Udet in her autobiography, even though he had been her mentor, flying companion, and friend for at least seven years.

Field Marshal Erhard Milch, who took over most of Udet's responsibilities as armaments chief for the Luftwaffe, was more concerned with the malignant agenda of the Third Reich than Udet had been. He had no interest in supporting the aerial adventures of a woman test pilot.

Hanna soon found a replacement for Udet's friendship and support in his friend Robert Ritter von Greim. However, Greim's support was limited because he was responsible for aerial combat operations first on the western front, then in the east against the Soviet Union. What support von Greim could not give Hanna, she obtained by appealing to higher authority. She never tired of inserting herself into flight test projects by exploiting her acquaintance with Hitler, claiming that the Fuehrer had given her license to fly the best and most-challenging aircraft the Third Reich had to offer.

Hanna Reitsch did most of her flying in gliders (sailplanes) during the 1930s. She demonstrated her skills in the Hirth *Habicht* (Hawk) on the opening day of the 1938 National Air Races at Cleveland, Ohio. Courtesy National Air and Space Museum, Smithsonian Institution, SI Neg. No. 94–7860.

Ernst Udet—World War I fighter ace, stunt pilot, airplane designer, and glider enthusiast—became Director General of Luftwaffe Equipment and Hanna Reitsch's friend and mentor. Courtesy National Archives, photo no. 242 HB–11790a2.

Hanna Reitsch charmed aircraft builder Herr Ernst Heinkel at a reception at the *Haus der Flieger* on 6 November 1937. Courtesy National Archives, photo no. 242–HLB–2334–3.

Hanna Reitsch proudly wore her Iron Cross, Second Class and Gold Medal for Military Flying accented with an encircling ring of diamonds. Courtesy National Air and Space Museum, Smithsonian Institution, SI Neg. No. 88–18695.

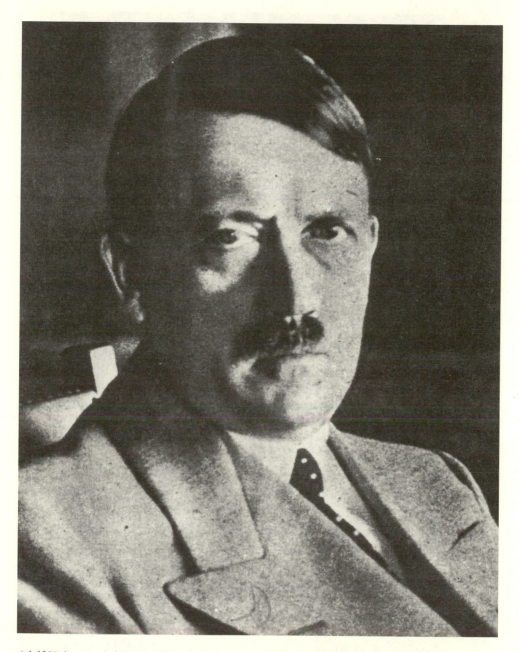

Adolf Hitler awarded Hanna Reitsch the Iron Cross, Second Class, on 28 March 1941 in recognition of her achievement as a test pilot. He soon became her patron, giving her access to fly any aircraft she wanted. A friendly relationship between the two lasted until the Fuehrer's death. Courtesy National Archives, photo no. 226–P–25–1854A.

Never one to be outdone, the flamboyant and corrupt Reich Marshal and Commander in Chief of the Luftwaffe, Hermann Goering, awarded Hanna Reitsch the Gold Medal for Military Flying, accented with an encircling ring of diamonds to complement her Iron Cross. The relationship between Reitsch and Goering would turn sour, in part, because of Hanna's friendship with Goering's rival, Robert Ritter von Greim. Courtesy National Archives, photo no. 242–HBA–5407.

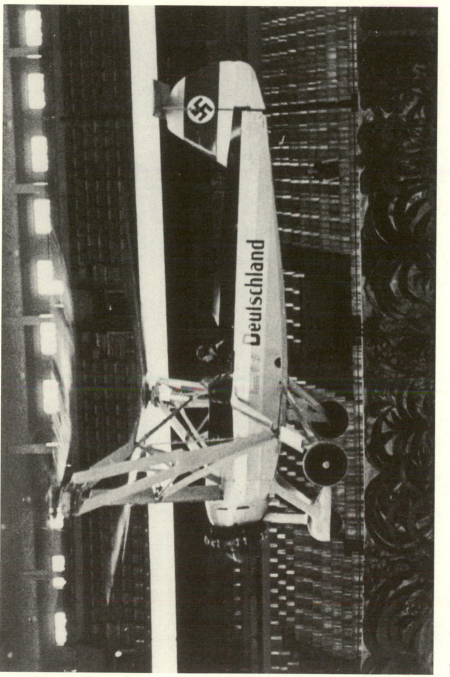

The Focke-Achgelis FW 61 *Hubschrauber* was the first practical helicopter. Hanna Reitsch flew it inside the Deutschlandhalle in Berlin at the Berlin Automobile Exposition in February 1938. Courtesy National Air and Space Museum, Smithsonian Institution, SI Neg. No. 95–2403.

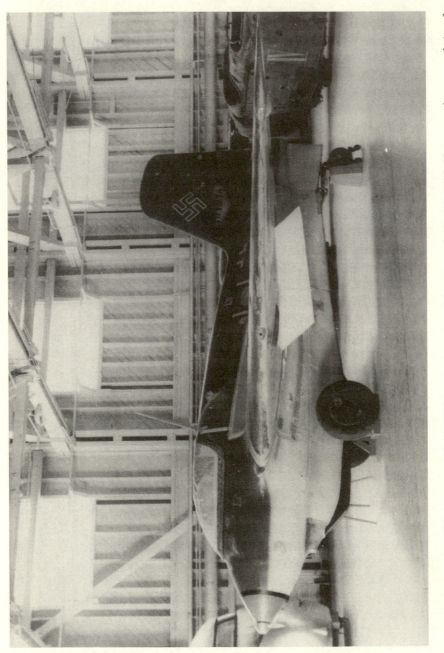

Hanna Reitsch exploited the patronage of Adolf Hitler to gain access to the Messerschmitt Me 163B *Komet*, a rocket-powered aircraft that nearly killed her in a crash landing. Courtesy National Air and Space Museum, Smithsonian Institution, SI Neg. No. 92–3599.

SS Major Otto Skorzeny collaborated with Hanna Reitsch to develop the "Suicide Bomb" project, Germany's equivalent of the Japanese *Kamikaze* weapons. The project never became operational. Courtesy National Archives, photo no. 226–P–25–12243.

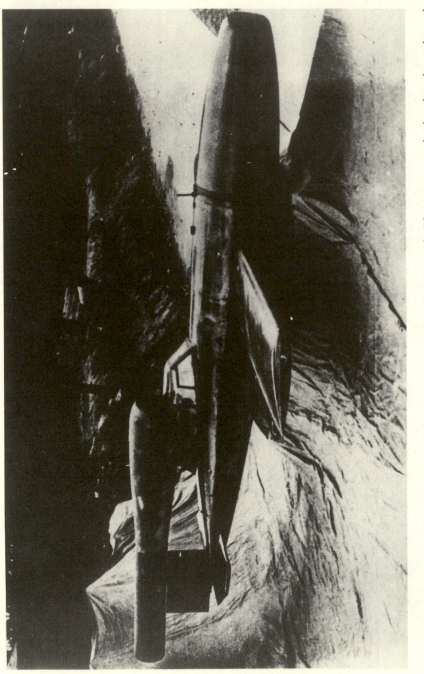

Hanna Reitsch flew the V-1 Reichenberg "Suicide Bomb," a pulse-jet-powered cruise missile. The weapon was developed too late to be used against Nazi Germany's enemies. Courtesy National Air and Space Museum, Smithsonian Institution, SI Neg. No. 92–3600.

Chapter 4

The Rocket Plane

Although Hanna Reitsch got a constant stream of high-visibility test-flying assignments while working for Hans Jacobs at the DFS, she was not its only test pilot; and Jacobs was not, by any means, the most imaginative designer there. Before taking over direction of conventional glider design work, Jacobs had been the assistant to Alexander Lippisch at the DFS. Lippisch was a man with a long history of unconventional and imaginative aircraft designs behind him. His test pilot during the middle 1930s and after was Heini Dittmar.[1] Although they worked separately at the DFS, Hanna's path would eventually join that of Lippisch and Dittmar with disastrous consequences for her. Before telling this story, some background is in order.

Alexander Lippisch produced his first radical, tailless glider designs in the mid-1920s. His success in designing gliders attracted the attention of Max Valier and Fritz von Opel, two rocket enthusiasts who hoped to wed rocket propulsion to an aircraft. Lippisch fitted solid-fueled rocket engines supplied by Valier and Opel to his tailless glider, the *Ente* ("Duck" in English). On 11 June 1928 the *Ente* was launched with the aid of a rubber shock cord, then its rocket engines were fired. The first flight lasted thirty-five seconds; a second flight lasted seventy seconds. When the *Ente* caught fire on the third flight, Opel and Valier went on to other adventures; and Lippisch dropped his momentary interest in rocket power.[2]

In the years that followed, Lippisch designed a series of tailless, delta-winged aircraft that soared as gliders and flew under the power of tractor and pusher propellers. This work culminated in a very successful aircraft powered by a tractor propeller, the DFS 39 Delta IVb. In late 1937, the success of this aircraft attracted the attention of Dr. Adolf Baeumker, Chief of the Air Ministry's research department. Dr. Baeumker ordered a modified DFS 39 Delta IVb with a lengthened fuselage, which would carry a "special power plant." Lippisch learned later to his chagrin that this power plant would be a liquid-fueled rocket motor. Production of this aircraft would be the beginning of the Reich Air Ministry's top secret *Projekt* X.[3]

Though progress was being made on the Air Ministry's DFS 39, the workshop at the DFS was simply not suitable for work under tight security. Furthermore, Lippisch and his group constantly found themselves taking a secondary position behind Hans Jacobs and his conventional, though highly successful, projects. Lippisch and his team resolved the problem by leaving the DFS to eventually settle at the Messerschmitt factory in Augsburg in January 1939.[4,5]

Development of Lippisch's rocket-powered aircraft almost came to an end in early 1940 when Hitler, projecting an early end to the war, banned all development projects that could not be completed within a year. To keep the project alive, Lippisch placed the liquid-fueled rocket engine into the DFS 194, an experimental aluminum and magnesium airframe, which, though never intended for rocket power, was ready to be used.[6] The DFS 194 had broad, swept-back wings with a span of about thirty feet and a fuselage about eighteen feet long. It had no tail, but it did have a vertical stabilizer with a split rudder, the halves positioned above and below the rocket exhaust.[7]

In August 1940 Heini Dittmar took the rocket-powered DFS 194 aloft at the Luftwaffe's test facility at Peenemuende on the Baltic coast where he reached an air speed of 341.8 miles per hour. Although Dittmar experienced some control problems at high speed, the flight was a stunning success.

The Reich Air Ministry was sufficiently impressed by the DFS 194 to raise the priority ranking of *Projekt* X. It approved production of three prototype aircraft designed from scratch to be rocket planes. The prototypes would be built at the Messerschmitt A. G. factory in Augsburg, where Lippisch and his team had moved in January 1939. The new aircraft would carry the name of the factory and be known as the Messerschmitt 163A, or the Me 163A.[6]

The first Me 163As were completed during the winter of 1941, and the flight test program was scheduled for the spring. The aircraft were of the same general shape and size as the DFS 194; but, being designed specifically to be powered by rocket engines, they were much sleeker beasts. The initial unpowered flight tests of an Me 163A were carried out near the Messerschmitt factory at Augsburg. With Heini Dittmar at the controls, the tiny aircraft was towed to altitude by a twin-engine Bf 110, then released.[8]

When General Ernst Udet, Director General of Luftwaffe Equipment (who had not yet taken his own life), arrived at the airfield one spring day in 1941, he found Alexander Lippisch outside the hangars watching the sky. Udet spotted the speck circling above, then pointed to it.

"What's that, Lippisch?"

"The Me 163," Lippisch answered.

The tiny tailless plane with swept-back wings dipped into a steep dive, and Udet's eyes followed it as it dropped like a falcon, plunging faster and faster toward the earth. It pulled out of the dive just over the airfield and flashed past Udet and Lippisch at well over 400 miles per hour. Then it pulled up sharply.

"What kind of engine has it?" Udet asked.

"None," Lippisch answered with a laugh.

The tiny aircraft with Heini Dittmar at the controls flashed by and pulled up again, stripping off speed with the maneuver. After several loops around the field, Dittmar brought his plane in for a landing.

"No engine! Impossible!" Udet grunted. Then he ran across the airfield to where Dittmar brought the plane to a stop.

Udet did a quick inspection of the craft and confirmed what Lippisch had told him. "It's true—there's no engine."

If the tiny aircraft could perform so fantastically without power, imagine what it could do with a rocket motor. Udet was sold. From then on he was the patron of the rocket plane, pushing for higher priority, watching *Projekt* X with keen interest.[8] After some design flaws were detected and corrected, Dittmar piloted the Me 163A in a dive to a top speed of 528 miles per hour, a remarkable achievement for any aircraft and doubly remarkable for one flying without a motor of any kind.

By the summer of 1941 the hydrogen peroxide-fueled rocket engine had been completed at the Walter Werke (factory) in Kiel, and both the engine and the Me 163A airframe were shipped to the Luftwaffe's test facility at Peenemuende. Engine and airframe were wedded, and Heini Dittmar made the first ground-launched, powered flight on 13 August 1941.[9] The aircraft, with Dittmar at the controls, quickly shattered all airspeed records. The speeds Dittmar reached climbed incrementally on each flight until he reached about 570 miles per hour, when the consumption of the fuel supply limited the top speed.[8]

The craft's designer, Alexander Lippisch, was not satisfied. He had calculated that the Me 163A could attain a top speed of 1,000 kilometers per hour (621 miles per hour) with 880 pounds of thrust at an altitude of 4,000 meters (13,120 feet), if it could get to that altitude. Heini Dittmar came up with the idea of towing the rocket plane to altitude, then assaulting its theoretical performance limit with an ample fuel supply. On 2 October 1941 the rocket plane was given a 75 percent fuel load, because the Bf 110 tow plane was not capable of towing the fully loaded Me 163A to altitude.[10]

When they reached 13,000 feet, Dittmar released the tow cable and fired the rocket motor. The pulsing power slammed him in the back as he pulled the stick back gently and began to climb. At 14,000 feet, Dittmar leveled off and let the power turn itself into speed. The speedometer on the instrument panel soon read 910 kilometers per hour and was still climbing; then it indicated over 1,000 kilometers per hour. Instrumentation on the ground also followed the rocket plane's speed, watching it climb until it peaked at 1,003 kilometers per hour (623.85 miles per hour or Mach 0.84).

Dittmar watched the airspeed indicator top the 1,000-kilometer-per-hour mark, then begin to waver. The laws of physics were beginning to take control of the tiny aircraft away from Dittmar. As the speed of the air passing over the wings increased, the center of lift migrated aft. When the plane passed the 1,000-kilometer-per-hour mark, the elevons at the back of the wings began to vibrate. The next moment, the lifting forces—now centered at the trailing edge of the wing—pitched the rocket plane into an uncontrollable dive.

With the aircraft accelerating downward faster than it would be drawn by gravity, negative "g" force threw Dittmar up against his shoulder straps and pulled the remaining fuel away from the pump. The rocket engine cut off. Dittmar wrestled with the machine, trying to bring it back under his control, thinking that he had lost it and was about to lose his life. Then just as suddenly as the plane had gone into the dive, control was back in Dittmar's hands. He eased the stick back, and the aircraft came out of its dive.

Dittmar's experience led him to make blunt evaluations of what he perceived as the limits of his aircraft and aeronautics. "The so-called Mach phenomenon that I had just experienced was the first knock on the door of the sound barrier which my aircraft had not been built to penetrate."[11] He added, "Flying beyond the mach [*sic*] barrier is impossible. Anyone who exceeds the barrier will probably end up shredded into thousands of pieces along with his ship. Flying much past the sound barrier can cost you your neck."[12]

Most of the officials of the Air Ministry back in Berlin received the news of Dittmar's speed record with skepticism; however, Ernst Udet was so enthusiastic that he demanded that the Me 163A be tooled up for mass production and fitted with weapons. Alexander Lippisch, however, knew the shortcomings of his experimental machine and explained to Udet the total impracticality of his proposal. In the end, Udet agreed to the development of a version of the rocket plane intended for combat, the Me 163B *Komet*.[13]

In April 1942 the Luftwaffe had begun to assign pilots to work with Lippisch and Dittmar on *Projekt* X. These men were combat veterans of the Battle of Britain and the invasions of Poland, France, and the Soviet Union. The first to be assigned was *Hauptmann* (Captain) Wolfgang Spaete, who would eventually become commanding officer of *Erprobungskommando* (Test Command) 16, the unit that would eventually bring the rocket plane into combat.

For the accomplishment of exceeding the speed of 1,000 kilometers per hour, Alexander Lippisch, designer of the airframe, Hellmuth Walter, designer of the rocket engine, and Heini Dittmar, pilot of the Me 163A, received the Lilienthal Trophy for Aeronautical Research, Germany's highest award for powered flight. Because of the war, of course, the speed record and the award were kept a state secret.[14] The world did not learn of Dittmar's achievement until long after the rocket planes had ceased to fly and Germany had been turned into rubble.

Nevertheless, anyone in experimental aeronautical circles in Germany knew that the Me 163A was the fastest aircraft in the air, and that its pilot, Heini Dittmar, was the fastest man on earth and the man to beat if one wanted to be the top pilot. Before his suicide, Ernst Udet probably told his protégée, Hanna Reitsch, all about the Me 163A and Dittmar's achievement. Hanna could not resist the thought of flying the rocket plane.

In late May 1942, Hanna Reitsch appeared at Augsburg with the intention of flying the Me 163B *Komet*, the successor to Dittmar's record-setting Me 163A. Whether she was there at the request of the Luftwaffe, by the invitation of Alexander Lippisch, or on her own initiative is not known. It is reported, though, that she had gotten permission from Alexander Lippisch to fly the new aircraft in tow. Heini Dittmar, who had known Hanna for nearly ten years and who had worked with her at the DFS, resented her intrusion into the flight test program. He was doubly irritated because, even before he knew of her arrival in Augsburg, she had been aloft in the Me 163A.

Dittmar bluntly offered his assessment of Hanna. "There are women who just can't stand it when a new man moves into town and they haven't gotten him in bed yet. Hanna is the same way about airplanes. As soon as a new airplane appears, she becomes obsessed with it and is not satisfied until she has flown it. O.K.—granted, this time it went fairly well. There was no accident and her goal had been achieved. But in my nightly prayers, I always include a little request that she doesn't show up again soon."[15]

But Hanna did not leave. Lippisch announced that she would share flight testing responsibilities with Dittmar. His decision was not prompted so much by confidence in her as a pilot, but by her connections. The gossip among the Luftwaffe pilots at Augsburg held that Lippisch was willing to take her on because he thought she could help him improve his position with the bureaucracy in Berlin and get a higher priority ranking. Dittmar, a civilian, had made it clear that he would quit rather than share the Me 163A and Me 163B with Hanna Reitsch.

The Luftwaffe pilots on the flight line were unanimous in holding that they would not get the Me 163B operational without Dittmar. Gossip spread among them alleging Hanna's lack of professionalism. One story told of how she let an aircraft she was to test sit for days while she waited for a call from someone of consequence at the Reich

Air Ministry; why she waited and from whom the call came were not mentioned.

In another tale, Hanna was found to have done an inadequate flight evaluation of a glider designed by Hans Jacobs at the DFS. The aircraft, the story went, had to be modified extensively afterward. One pilot had the following evaluation of her in light of this incident:

> "Although Hanna Reitsch is a smart and clever pilot, she flys [sic] with her heart and not with her brains—at least without critical understanding of her work. She's one of those types of pilots who get the most impossible airplane up into the air, and then tells the design engineers that the plane is flyable. And when somebody else detects a deficiency, the design engineer is highly surprised and the uncritical pilot [i.e., Hanna Reitsch] is deeply offended."[16]

The head of the Luftwaffe's Test Command 16, the group that would bring the Me 163B *Komet* to operational status, was Captain Wolfgang Spaete. Spaete had known Hanna Reitsch when he was on the staff of the DFS, and he had competed against her in many glider competitions. Spaete had the following evaluation of Hanna Reitsch: "Her pride would neither tolerate accepting us as co-workers nor even asking us for professional advice. She was Number One. She knew it all!"[16]

How much truth there was in these criticisms leveled at Hanna by the male pilots is not known. What is obvious, though, is that they did not want her as part of their group. Wolfgang Spaete came up with a compromise solution that would satisfy Lippisch by allowing Hanna to fly the Me 163B and would also keep her away from Heini Dittmar, thereby keeping him on the team.[16] Messerschmitt's factory at Oberstraubling, near Regensburg, had been charged with building 70 Me 163B production units.[17] Dittmar would continue to conduct flights at Augsburg, and Hanna would be assigned to Oberstraubling to make acceptance flights of the aircraft produced there.[16]

In October 1942, Heini Dittmar was flying an Me 163A prototype, which had been fitted with improved landing flaps. His landing appeared to be normal; but after a few minutes, those who had seen the landing from the hangar walked over to the airplane to see what was keeping Dittmar. They found him sitting, paralyzed with pain. After a lengthy investigation of the accident, it was still not clear if Dittmar's injuries were the result of the impact of landing, malfunctioning shock absorbers, or the rough ride that followed. However, as a safety measure, the pilot's seat was redesigned with additional springing to better absorb the shock of landing.[18,19]

Heini Dittmar spent the next year and a half recovering from severe injuries to his back and spinal cord.[20] With Dittmar out of action, Hanna Reitsch became more valuable to the *Projekt* X flight test program.

At Oberstraubling, near Regensburg, Hanna Reitsch wasted no time in getting into the cockpit of the rocket planes. By late October 1942, she made three flights in the prototype Me 163A and one in the first Me 163B *Komet* to be produced. This aircraft, which was designated Me 163B V1, was really just the airframe with no motor, fuel tanks, or special equipment. It was a very light aircraft with a landing speed of 85 knots. Her next flight was to be in an Me 163B designated Me 163B V5, still without its rocket motor, but with a gun sight, cannon, and with a full load of electronic and radio equipment. It landed at 115 knots.[21]

Hanna had been thrilled by her first flights in the planes, especially the Me 163A under rocket power. "To fly the rocket plane Me 163," she later said, "was to live through a fantasy of Munchhausen [Germany's legendary, thirteenth century teller of fantastic tales]. One took off with a roar and a sheet of flame, then shot steeply upward to find oneself the next moment in the heart of the empyrean."[22]

On this fall day, 30 October 1942,[21] Hanna sat at the controls of the redesigned, combat version of the rocket plane, the Me 163B V5, waiting for the tow plane to pull it into the air for a glide test from the airfield at Oberstraublin. If the plane performed according to specifications, the plant would turn it over to the Luftwaffe.[23]

The aircraft's fuselage was a projectile eighteen feet eight inches long with a rounded plexiglass canopy. Its wings were essentially the same as those of its predecessors, the DFS 194 and the prototype Me 163A: a broad, swept-back slab thirty feet six inches wide. A vertical stabilizer split the air at the end of the pudgy fuselage. Also, like its predecessors, the aircraft would roll to a takeoff on wheels that would fall away shortly after it became airborne. The plane was designed to land on a shock-absorbing skid slung below its belly. The rocket engine, when it would be installed, was intended to be improved in power and reliability over the 80 percent hydrogen peroxide (*T-Stoff*)-fueled Walter HWK 509 used in the prototype Me 163A. The new engine, the Walter HWK 109–509, would use *T-Stoff* to burn a mixture of methyl alcohol, hydrazine, and water (*C-Stoff*). The thrust of the new engine was intended to be controllable by the pilot from 220 pounds (100 kilograms) while idling to a terrifying 3,307 pounds (1,500 kilograms) at full power.[24]

Because of its military mission, the cockpit of the Me 163B was significantly different from that of its prototype, the Me 163A. To begin with, it was roomy, wide enough to accommodate a 13-gallon tank for explosive and corrosive *T-Stoff* on each side of the pilot's seat. Behind the pilot's seat was a sheet of armor eight millimeters thick. The pilot was protected at the front by the plane's nose cone made of 15-millimeter-thick armor and by a ninety-millimeter-thick bulletproof glass shield under the canopy and above the instrument panel. The final touch, clearly defining the military mission of the rocket plane, was a Revi 16B gun sight mounted to the base of the bulletproof glass shield.[25]

The cockpit of the Me 163B, like that of most aircraft, was not built to the needs of Hanna's diminutive proportions. It was, in fact, quite wide because the fuselage tanks had to be large enough to hold 6,500 pounds of fuel. Even average-size male pilots had to loosen their shoulder straps just to be able to lean to the side and see the ground. Hanna adapted to the cockpit by using a thick back cushion so that she could sit forward; she did not hook up the shoulder straps. Even so, she could barely reach the rudder pedals. There had been a plan to put blocks on the pedals, like one would put on the pedals of a bicycle for a small child; but they had not been installed by the time of her flight. Hanna had to put her body through contortions just to move the rudder.[21]

Whether or not the aircraft was ready for her, Hanna was ready for it. She looked over the gun sight and through the bulletproof glass at the twin-engine Bf 110 that was to tow her and her airplane to an unpowered, uneventful glide test. The tow plane revved its engines, the cable came taught, and the tiny rocket plane began to roll down the runway. In a few seconds the twin-engine tow plane was airborne, the Me 163B with Hanna at its controls right behind. As her plane was approaching an altitude of thirty feet, Hanna moved the lever that would release the wheeled undercarriage. The plane began to shake violently as if it had hit a turbulent airflow. Hanna was in trouble, and she knew it. She tried to contact the tow plane by radio: no response. The radio was not working, and Hanna's tiny plane was still going through sickening shudders.

In the gun turret of the Bf 110 tow plane, Hanna saw a man waving something white, a handkerchief or scarf. She saw the landing gear of the tow plane lower, then retract. The gear lowered, then retracted again. Hanna understood the problem. The wheeled undercarriage of her tiny craft had not fallen away. It was still suspended from the belly of her plane, disrupting the air flow around the plane and causing it to shake like a bad hangover.[26]

The pilot of the tow plane, Rudolf Opitz, was following standard operating procedure. He flew broad circles around the airfield and gradually gained altitude. The trips "round the ring" took time and gave everybody a chance to get acquainted with the characteristics of the misbehaving aircraft. At last, the linked pair bounced their heads against the bottom of the cloud base at 10,500 feet, and Hanna released the umbilical that held her to the mother plane.[23,26]

Now with the tiny craft under her control—as much as it was under anybody's control—Hanna pulled up sharply, hoping to break free the stuck undercarriage. The violent vibrations continued: The undercarriage was still in place.

Should she bail out and let the plane smash itself into a jumble of shattered plywood and twisted aluminum, or should she wrestle the unruly bird to the ground? Landing the plane would not be easy, but it could be done. After all, the world's greatest aviatrix was at the controls. Hanna hoped that the undercarriage was hanging exactly where it had been when she taxied the plane on its takeoff. She would take the chance that when she touched down, the undercarriage would not tear loose and rip through the fuselage. She would trust the luck that had kept her alive and unhurt through all of the risky flights she had made in her life. She began the long, spiral glide down to the airfield.

Without power, Hanna had at most one chance to bring the airplane to a safe landing. She approached the runway high, then side slipped the last hundred yards to strip off excess altitude. The wheels under the fuselage, now turned slightly to the side, dug into the air and plowed ragged air currents over the control surfaces. The plane stalled, then fell like a duck full of bird-shot.[26]

From the tow plane, Rudolf Opitz watched the unpowered aircraft. He did not see the violent shuddering of the rocket plane, nor did he notice that it had stalled. The Me 163B appeared to make a normal landing—albeit with rapid deceleration—on a plowed field. Hanna's aircraft came to a stop just a few yards from her target runway.[23]

Hanna had the clear impression that the airplane had somersaulted—though it had not—when it hit the plowed ground. She was surprised that she was sitting upright rather than hanging upside-down from her harness. With her right hand she reached over to open the plexiglass canopy. Surprise: It was intact. She ran her right hand down her left arm and hand, then slowly along her sides, across her chest, and down her legs. Surprise again: Everything was there; nothing seemed to be broken; she felt no pain. Then she noticed a stream of blood dribbling down her flight suit. Calmly she traced it back to its source, moving her fingers across her face.

Her nose was gone. In its place was a ragged fissure that pumped out sticky bubbles every time she exhaled. She turned her head to the side; her vision faded. She had something to do before she blacked out. She pulled a pad of paper and pencil from a pocket and drew a sketch, recording her recollections of the approach and landing. Then, as the rescue party approached the plane, she did something uniquely feminine. She took out a handkerchief and tied it over the lower half of her shattered face. As she explained later, she wanted to spare her rescuers the shock of seeing her bloodied condition. Then the black clouds closed in again.[26]

Hanna had done her job by bringing back her aircraft undamaged. She might have walked away from her hard landing without a scratch if she had paid attention to simple details. She had ignored the most basic safety precaution and failed to wear her shoulder straps, and she had not bothered to stow away the useless gun sight that was mounted to the base of the bulletproof glass shield only inches in front of her nose. Without the security of the shoulder straps, she was thrown face-first into the gun sight, which she could have easily stowed before takeoff.[27]

Wolfgang Spaete, who had viewed Hanna critically before her crash, developed a respect for her dedication and strength of will as a result of her behavior. He reported, "To this day, I know of no other case where a badly injured pilot didn't first take care of his injuries and then, much later, after he had some time to think, write out his accident report."

Those at the scene also added details revealing the iron will of Hanna Reitsch. By the time they had reached the rocket plane, she had regained consciousness and opened the aircraft's canopy. One of the men lifted Hanna from the cockpit and offered to place her on the ground, where someone had put a piece of clothing as ground cover. She refused. She insisted on walking back to the airfield, although she accepted the support of someone's arm. At the edge of the airfield she got into a car and was driven to the factory's first-aid room. When the doctor there had done all he could, she refused to be taken to the hospital in an ambulance but got into a car instead. At the hospital, she refused to use the main entrance. Instead she insisted on walking up four flights to the doctor's suite. Only then did she consent to notifying the hospital staff that she had arrived. She said that she did not want to make a big fuss over her crash.[28]

After Hanna's flight, it was discovered that the outcome could have been worse; the aircraft could have been destroyed in flight and Hanna killed. There was too much play in the bolts and assemblies that attached the wings to the fuselage. Had Hanna been able to take the aircraft beyond moderate airspeed—which she was prevented from doing because of the attached wheeled undercarriage—it might have broken up in flight. When this defect was detected, all seventy rocket planes built at the Oberstraubling factory were grounded. Hanna's was the first and last flight of an Me 163B *Komet* that had been built there.[29]

Chapter 5

Recovery and Return

Hanna Reitsch was in critical condition. The X ray of her skull reminded one of Humpty-Dumpty after the fall. There were four fractures in the basal area and two fractures in the facial area; the upper jawbones were displaced, and the bones of the nose were separated. Her brain had been compressed. The surgeon did his best.

When Hanna awoke, her head was completely bandaged; only the blue, bruised outlines of her eyes and her swollen lips poked through holes in the white mass. She could see that she was in a bright, friendly room. There were smiling faces, one of them her aunt's. To Hanna, they seemed strangely concerned. The following day, Hanna's mother arrived to take up the long vigil at her bedside.[1]

Hanna asked to see her close friend, Edelgard vom Berg, a woman whom Hanna had known since they both attended medical school in Kiel[2] and who was a surgeon in Berlin. Hanna believed her friend would be more candid with her about her condition than were the doctors at the hospital. Vom Berg left Berlin by car, but she never arrived in Regensburg. She died in an automobile accident, and Hanna received the news as a devastating blow.[1]

A few days after Hanna's accident, while she lay in the Hospital of the Sisters of Mercy in Regensburg, she was awarded the Iron Cross, First Class, one grade higher than the Second Class medal she already possessed.[1] Her country loved her even though she had nearly killed herself due to her own recklessness. It remained to be seen whether she would collect the medal in person or posthumously. Best wishes, flowers, and gifts poured in from friends, acquaintances, and admirers. Heinrich Himmler, Reichsfuehrer of the SS and chief of the Gestapo, sent a slab of chocolate and a bottle of fruit juice with a personal letter of encouragement. He periodically sent additional gifts accompanied by handwritten notes while Hanna was in the hospital.[3] Wolfgang Spaete went to visit Hanna with a bouquet of flowers. He was met by Hanna's mother, who accepted the flowers but turned him away. Hanna did not want anyone to see her in her battered and bandaged condition.[4]

Hanna asked about her condition. It was obvious that her condition was serious, and she wanted to know how serious. Should she prepare herself for . . . the end? The doctors were evasive: a bad sign. Endless day blended into endless day as Hanna lay in bed, her head cradled in soft pillows. She brooded over her physical condition, which did not seem to change. Would she ever leave the hospital? Would she ever fly again? Her only comfort was her mother at her side, calming her, urging her to abandon herself to God's will. Emy Reitsch knew that only God's love could save Hanna and let her fly again.[1]

Hanna was also depressed by rumors that spread in February 1943 about the disaster on the eastern front.[5] Nearly 200,000 men had been lost at Stalingrad, 91,000 soldiers had been taken prisoner, and barely 5,000 of them would survive the Siberian POW camps.[6] The direction of the war had changed, and the German people began to understand that Germany would pay for its aggression.

In March 1943, five months after her crash, Hanna was discharged from the hospital in Regensburg. Her bandages had been removed; the bruises had faded; the swelling had subsided; the torn skin had mended. Still obviously weak, she would need a much longer convalescence before she could return to anything that resembled a normal life. The doctors had done an admirable job of restoring her face, of putting Humpty-Dumpty back together again. But there were some things the doctors could not do. Nobody could give her the will or the ability to fly again; she must find these within herself.[1]

She never told anyone about the constant ache in her head, or that the gentlest motion like that of a car or a train made her nauseous and dizzy.

After spending a few days at her parents' home in Hirschberg, Silesia, Hanna went to the unoccupied summer home of friends. The house was near Saalburg, in an isolated idyllic area halfway up a mountainside. Her only companions were a club and a pistol that she brought along for protection. Her goal was to regain her strength and her precious sense of balance, both essential if she was ever to fly again.

She began by climbing: a stairway that led to the gabled roof of the house, paths that led to the mountain ridge, trees. At first the least effort left her exhausted, and her head throbbed with an agonizing ache; but through determination and persistence, she regained her strength. She was soon sitting on top of the gabled roof, at the mountain ridge, or high in a pine tree surveying the landscape below. She had arrived in early April, and four weeks later she was able to do all this without suffering any dizziness.

Without the permission of her doctors, but with the assistance of the commander of a School of Aerial Warfare at Breslau, she began to fly again. At first she piloted a glider, then powered aircraft. Through strength of will, she put the airplane through spins, dives, and acrobatics. Within a few weeks, according to her own judgment, she was flying as well as she had before her accident. She was ready to return to challenge the rocket plane that had nearly killed her.[7]

Soon after Hanna reported back to duty with the Luftwaffe, she received an invitation from Reich Marshal Hermann Goering to join him and his wife for lunch at their residence in Obersalzberg.[5] At one time a dynamic leader of the Nazi cause, a personality to be reckoned with, Hermann Goering had by his self-indulgence become—though nobody would risk saying it—a liability to the Third Reich. He was a drug addict and had become corpulent. He was vain and fond of wearing makeup and ostentatious attire. In the moments when he was not serving the Third Reich, and these moments seemed to be increasing, he amassed a collection of the finest stolen art treasures in Europe. He lived more lavishly than any of the other leaders of the Third Reich.[8,9]

Not surprisingly, when Hanna Reitsch and Hermann Goering met at Obersalzberg, they discussed Hanna's crash and the rocket plane. As they talked, Hanna realized that Goering believed the Me 163B was being mass produced and would reach combat soon. Hanna attempted to set him straight: The aircraft was still in the experimental stage. Goering was insulted by Hanna's affront to his belief and stalked out of the room. His wife went after him, smoothed over his ruffled feathers, and brought him back. The remainder of their luncheon was awkward for all. Goering would not give up his illusion, and Hanna would not give up the blunt truth. It was the last time Hanna Reitsch and Hermann Goering saw each other.[5]

In the Third Reich, one could not have too many friends, especially if one wanted to fly the most-advanced aircraft and found oneself in a strained relationship with the chief of the Luftwaffe, Hermann Goering. In July 1943 Hanna visited the man who had sent her small gifts and handwritten notes of encouragement while she was in the hospital, Reichsfuehrer of the SS and head of the Gestapo, Heinrich Himmler.[10]

By virtue of his positions, Himmler was the enforcer of the Third Reich's most-vile domestic policies, which ranged from suppression of political dissidents to extermination of the Jews. Furthermore, his bizarre attempt at social engineering, the *Lebensborn* program, encouraged the mating of attractive "Aryan" women to equally "superior" SS men for the purpose of breeding a master race. This was done, of course, without benefit of love, marriage, or permanent relationship; and the *Lebensborn* program outraged anyone with even a trace of moral decency who learned about it.[11]

In the Reitsch household, Himmler was viewed as an enemy of Christianity. In light of later revelations of his outrageous criminal activities, this would seem almost a compliment. Yet after Hanna received the kind attentions of Himmler, her mother began to rethink her attitude about the Reichsfuehrer. Perhaps they were judging the man too harshly. After all, all they knew about him was how he conducted his official duties for the Reich. Hanna's mother encouraged her to visit Himmler and thank him personally for his kindness.

Hanna arrived at Himmler's East Prussian headquarters and was met by the Reichsfuehrer. Himmler's appearance was innocuous. He had thinning hair and wore metal-rimmed glasses. He looked more like a school teacher or an accountant than what he was, the most ruthless man in Nazi Germany. They had a comfortable dinner with a group senior SS officers, then Hanna and Himmler went to his study for a private conversation. Hanna candidly told him that his name and reputation had always caused "trepidation" in her family. He chided her for judging people hastily.

They talked about religious beliefs. Hanna believed; Himmler, apparently expert in matters of theology, did not. They discussed the *Lebensborn* program, and Himmler claimed that his intentions had been misunderstood. He respected and valued women, he said; he was considering introduction of a *Stabshelferinnen* (staff assistance) organization into the SS. Women would then have a place, albeit doing subservient clerical work, in his elite organization.[10]

They spoke for several hours; and by the end, Hanna had to admit that Himmler's manners were impeccable. In viewing the furnishings of his study, she also judged that he had simple but superb taste. Himmler gave her a tour, and Hanna was particularly taken by the engravings that lined the walls. Himmler showed Hanna a Christmas platter that was being produced by a firm called Allach; he had contributed to the design himself. When he asked her what she thought of it, she told him she did not like it. Himmler puzzled over Hanna's comment for a moment, then said he would cancel the order for its production.[10] Himmler apparently failed to mention that Allach-Munich, Ltd., the company that produced the Christmas platter, exploited slave labor from the Dachau concentration camp to produce its fine porcelain pieces.[12]

While Hanna was convalescing, Test Command 16, the Luftwaffe group charged with bringing the Me 163B *Komet* to combat status, had moved the center of its operations from the Messerschmitt factory at Augsburg to the Luftwaffe's experimental aircraft base at Peenemuende.[13] Peenemuende was located on the northern end of Usedom Island on the sparsely populated shores of the Baltic Sea. It encompassed two side-by-side weapons-research stations operated by the Luftwaffe and the German Army respectively. The Army's rocket research and development center was at the northeastern end of the island, and the Luftwaffe's advanced aircraft test facility was at the northwestern end.

Hanna followed the rocket-plane group to the Luftwaffe's facility at Peenemuende-West, and while there on 17 August 1943, she visited old friends at the Army facility. After dinner, Hanna sat in the Hearth Room of the mess, the main social gathering place of the Army facility. She was with the men who were creating Nazi Germany's most sophisticated and terrifying new weapon, the A-4 rocket, later known as the V-2 ballistic missile.

The group's leader was General Walter Dornberger, who, at nearly forty-eight, was the old man of the team. Dornberger found Hanna to be "elegant, energetic, clear-headed, and courageous." "Whenever anything brought her to Peenemuende we were always glad to see her," he said. Dornberger recalled that Hanna wore a dark blue uniform—one of her own design because she was not a formal member of any military organization. On it she had pinned her Iron Cross, First Class and her gem-encrusted Gold Medal for Military Flying. She sat comfortably curled in a deep arm chair.[14]

Second in order of authority was Wernher von Braun, the civilian technical director of the Army's rocket development program and the man generally given credit for being the brains behind designing the V-2. After the war, he would come to the United States and become a leader of the American space program. Von Braun, like Hanna, was from Silesia. Both were thirty-one years old. They had met in 1932 when both were taking an advanced course in glider flying at the Grunau Training School.[15]

A third member of the group was Ernst Steinhoff. He was thirty-one years old, had worked as a pilot for the DFS, and held the rank of Flugkapitan. At that time, he also held the world's record for distance in a glider. While at the DFS, Steinhoff had written his doctoral dissertation on aviation instruments. He had left the DFS to join the Army's rocket development team as head of the guidance and control division under von Braun.[16]

Not surprisingly, a major topic of discussion that evening was flying. The evening of good fellowship broke up around 11:30 P.M. as Dornberger went to the guest house he used when at Peenemuende, and Steinhoff went home to his wife and three children at the residential area to the south. Von Braun escorted Hanna to the car that would take her back to the visitors' quarters at the Luftwaffe's Peenemuende-West base.[17]

The first sign that something was not right appeared in the night sky nine and a half minutes after midnight. A red marker flare bloomed over the Army base; one minute later sixteen more flares illuminated Peenemuende with a cold white glow. Moments later, the 497 bombers of the RAF's "Operation Hydra" began their attack. For over an hour, they flew a north-to-south pattern over the Army's rocket development base blasting parts of it to rubble, setting other parts on fire. A huge blaze engulfed the pine forest in which the base was situated. Inexplicably, the RAF did not target the Luftwaffe's base just to the west.[18,19]

When the attack was over and the last RAF bomber had escaped from the defending Luftwaffe fighters, much of the rocket base had been damaged; but it had not been put out of action. Hanna Reitsch and her dinner companions all survived. The 735 killed were almost all civilians; 178 men, women, and children had died at the housing settlement. Most of the rest of the casualties were slave laborers, Poles and Russians who had been trapped in the Trassenheide labor camp. They had been conscripted to do construction work for the conqueror of their homelands.[20]

The air raid on Peenemuende was probably not Hanna's first experience with the horror of an Allied attack on her homeland. However, it probably was her first actual experience of the devastation the Third Reich's enemies could cause. Hanna knew Germany could look forward to more and worse attacks, and she wanted to do something about it.

The ashes of Peenemuende had not yet cooled when Hanna found herself in Berlin having lunch at the Flying Club with two old friends in August 1943. Later, when she recounted the occasion, she did not name her friends but only described them as "an aeronautical medical specialist" and "a very skillful and experienced glider pilot." Not surprisingly, the conversation centered on the war, which was going badly, and the bleak future Germany faced should it be defeated. At the end of the First World War, Germany had been humiliated and impoverished by the victors. It seemed obvious that Germany could expect even worse treatment the second time around. Germany's only hope would be to force a negotiated peace and to do so quickly.

Lunch was forgotten as they speculated on what they could do to turn the tide. They were technicians, not foot soldiers; so, not surprisingly, they saw Germany's salvation in technology. They were also individuals who viewed themselves as—although they did not use the word—courageous. They began to formulate a plan that used technology and required brave pilots.

The Allies, they reasoned, could only be brought to the bargaining table to end the war if their military strength was considerably weakened. Germany would have to hit its enemies hard and fast by destroying power stations, water supplies, and factories. In the event of an invasion of the European continent, the targets would be naval and merchant ships. The only realistic way of doing this was to strike from the air with pilots guiding explosive cargos to the centers of their targets. Germany, they concluded, needed suicide bombers.

It did not take the three visionaries long to discover that Germany was full of zealots like themselves who were enthusiastic about the possibility of sacrificing their lives for the protection of Hitler's Reich and for the salvation of their wives and children and country.

Hanna took the plan for "Operation Suicide" to Field Marshal Milch, Deputy Chief of the Luftwaffe and Goering's second-in-command, to recruit his support in getting the missing components. Milch's reaction was immediate and unequivocal. He did not see suicide missions as being compatible with the German mentality. He refused to consider the proposal. Period. Their meeting was over.

Hanna was disappointed that she could not persuade Milch that such an act of self-sacrifice, as she described it, to save the lives of one's countrymen, was completely justifiable. Her backup position was that the choice should be left to the pilots, but Milch did not let her get that far. Many years later, after the war, Hanna still believed that she and her friends had been misunderstood. The plan was logical, pure in its idealism, and completely rational. Hanna was not deterred by Milch's rejection. If he would not support their plan for "Operation Suicide," she would take it to a higher authority. Until an opportunity to do so presented itself to her, she still had hopes of mastering the rocket plane that had nearly killed her.[21]

Soon after the bombing of Peenemuende in August, Test Command 16 found itself a new and safer home at Bad Zwischenahn, a short distance from the North Sea in the northwest corner of Germany.[22,23] Production versions of the Me 163B *Komet* were expected soon, and pilots were arriving to test the aircraft and fly it in combat. The flight training program began with docile unpowered gliders and worked its way up to the rocket planes. A small number of the relatively well-behaved prototypes, the Me 163As, were available. Only when a pilot showed he could command the flight of the Me 163A would he be allowed to fly the combat-equipped, flaming terror of the skies, the Me 163B.[24]

In mid-December 1943 the commanding officer of Test Command 16, Captain Wolfgang Spaete, was told by one of his subordinates that he had received an unexpected Christmas present: Hanna Reitsch had arrived at Bad Zwischenahn. She had no orders sending her there, the man told Spaete. She simply said that she had a blanket author-ization from Hitler to fly any aircraft she might find in Germany. Not wanting to take the chance that Hanna might really have Hitler's blessing, Spaete's subordinate let Hanna be checked out in the rocket plane.

Later that day, Spaete visited flight operations to see if what he had been told was true, and, sure enough, there she was in happy conversation with his apprentice rocket-plane warriors. Spaete was not pleased. He called higher authorities in Berlin to find out what he could do about his uninvited guest. He was advised to let her fly as long as she did not interfere with operations.[25]

Hanna lived with the members of Test Command 16 as a soldier among soldiers.[26] She ate at the mess with the other pilots, dining on some of the best food available in Germany: eggs, toast made from real white bread, meat, real tea, and coffee. The superb food that had disappeared from most tables long ago was not a perk for the elite pilots of the Luftwaffe's most technically advanced unit. It was an "altitude diet," as Dr. Dunker, an expert on high-altitude flying, ex-plained ominously. It was formulated to avoid hard-to-digest and flat-ulence-promoting foods. Without the diet, the rocket plane pilots' bellies would blow up like toy balloons when they blasted from the earth to altitudes nearing 40,000 feet in a little over three and a half minutes. Such a distraction could be deadly during aerial combat.[27]

An essential tool of the rocket pilots' training at Bad Zwischenahn was the "rocket laundry," a chamber that simulated high altitude by reducing air pressure. It was a steel chamber about half the size of a railroad car with one door that could just as easily have been on a bank vault. Before they could fly the rocket plane, all pilots were required to take daily "rides" in the "rocket laundry." Hanna took her place with the men sitting at the long table inside the chamber.[26]

The exercise had the dual purpose of acclimating the pilots to high altitude flight and teaching them to recognize the symptoms of "al-titude sickness." Altitude sickness was the consequence of oxygen deprivation, which would result if the aircraft's oxygen system mal-functioned. Oxygen deprivation did strange things to the mind, which, if not corrected quickly by a fast dive to low altitude, would lead to fatal consequences.[28]

The "rocket laundry" had been validated by tests done with pris-oners at the Dachau concentration camp. They had "flown" in a similar high-altitude chamber at Dachau to simulated altitudes as high as 68,000 feet. About eighty prisoners paid for the trips with their lives.[29,30] Most of the rocket pilots, including Hanna, did not know that the parameters of their exercise had been worked out at the expense of enemies of the Reich. An exception was Wolfgang Spaete, who had learned of the experiments at Dachau from Heinrich Himmler. Himmler, it seems, was quite proud of his imagined contribution to aeronautical research.[31]

By the end of 1943, novice rocket-pilots of Test Command 16 were graduating to sharp starts of the Me 163B, that is, rocket-powered takeoffs from the ground. The takeoffs went smoothly for the most part, although there were annoying accidents. Accidents were bound to happen, especially with a radically new aircraft.

One pilot, for example, failed to lift off, and his plane skidded over the airfield in wide turns. The pilot jumped clear of the runaway aircraft moments before it blew up.

A pilot named Walter was beneath the canopy of an Me 163B preparing for takeoff. A "fantastic hiss" came from the fighter. The sound was wrong. Heads turned. Too late. The sleek aircraft turned into a monstrous fireball, and the shock of the explosion slammed through the air.

"Walter!" somebody yelled. Men in flying suits, feet in fur boots were pounding toward the flames.

When they reached the flight line, they found smoke still rising from the dark greasy stain that covered the ground. Twisted scraps of metal littered the pavement. Walter was gone—almost. Where the sleek new aircraft had been, they found a jagged piece of metal. Smeared on it were a few traces of bloody flesh and a snow-white fragment of bone. Eighty meters away a mechanic found a naked leg, severed just below the knee.

Before long a medical crew arrived. They placed the bone fragment and the severed leg on a stretcher, then they searched the area for anything else that might have once been part of Walter. After 15 minutes of fruitless searching, they loaded the stretcher into an ambulance and drove away.[32]

The day after Walter's violent death, Captain Wolfgang Spaete met with Hanna Reitsch. (Wolfgang Spaete says they met in her quarters;[33] Mano Ziegler says the meeting took place in Spaete's office.[34])

Spaete began by asking Hanna if she was satisfied with the flying opportunities she had been given at Bad Zwischenahn.

Hanna admitted that she was pleased with her accommodations and the flying experiences that she had been given—as far as they went; but, she told Spaete, she wanted to fly the operational version of the Me 163B.

Spaete, trying to sound fatherly, told her that he could not give her that opportunity.

Hanna became upset. She had prepared herself to fly the operational rocket-plane, she said. She had Hitler's authorization.

Spaete pointed out that he had heard the story about the Fuehrer's authorization, but he had not seen it in writing. He had allowed Hanna to fly his group's aircraft out of good will, but he was not going to take the chance that something unfortunate might happen to her. The accident of the previous day hovered over the conversation like the pink mist that had once been the pilot Walter.

"We're at war!" Hanna argued. "One victim more or less, won't change anything! Sacrifices have to be made."

Spaete disagreed. He wanted to avoid more sacrifices, such as Walter's. He reminded Hanna that their two new aircraft were for operational tests. "They are supposed to be evaluated for their operational suitability by fighter pilots," he said. "You can't do that because you have never flown a single combat mission against the enemy."[35]

Spaete conveniently failed to remember that Heini Dittmar, the Me 163's first test pilot, was a civilian who had never flown in combat. Furthermore, *Oberleutnant* (Flying Officer) Rudolf Opitz, Dittmar's successor as chief test pilot,[36] had an irrelevant combat record: He had piloted the DFS-230 transport glider during the invasion of Belgium.[37]

Hanna tried charm. "Wolfgang, we ought to work together as friends!"

"Come on back in three months and we'll talk about it again."

"Is that your last word?"

"That's my last word."[35]

Lieutenant Mano Ziegler had seen Hanna leaving the office of his commanding officer, Captain Wolfgang Spaete, as he was entering. The normally gregarious Hanna had brushed past him. Ziegler thought she might have had tears in her eyes. Ziegler reported to

Spaete on the plans for Walter's funeral, then followed Hanna to her room. She answered on the third knock.

Ziegler found Hanna on her bed, crying.

"For goodness sake, What's the matter, Hanna?"

It was a few moments before she controlled her sobs enough to speak.

"Spaete has forbidden me to fly tomorrow, and it was all arranged! Oh, it's all so mean!"

So that's all there was to it? Ziegler was relieved.

"He knows very well that I have longed for this take-off ever since my accident. And now he slams the door in front of my nose. It is so unfair!"

Ziegler asked why Spaete had decided to not let her fly the rocket plane.

"It could be *too* dangerous! He says that he is not prepared to take the responsibility in case something should happen to me. As if I have ever asked if a flight will be dangerous or not! It is just because I am a woman! Oh no! Women are not good enough to fly the Komet!"

"But you have flown before, Hanna."

"Towed starts only—do you call *that* flying?"

"But you have made rocket take-offs in the Me 163A, haven't you?"

"Of course I have, but the 'A' is not the 'B', and I want . . . I will fly the 'B'! I shall go straight to see Goering—today, now!"

Hanna pulled out her suitcase and began throwing her things into it. Her tears had dried up, and a look of determination had come to her face. When she finished packing, she slammed her suitcase shut.

"Give my regards to all our comrades, Mano," she said. "Thank them all for the wonderful days that I have spent here with them at Bad Zwischenahn. I shall never forget them!"[33]

In the weeks that followed, Wolfgang Spaete heard reports that Hanna Reitsch had not quietly accepted his decision about not letting her fly the Me 163B. She was, apparently, working her way up the Luftwaffe hierarchy trying to find an ally who would strong-arm Spaete into letting her fly the rocket plane. One general advised that the choice of letting her fly the rocket plane was his, but "to leave her [Hanna] alone as best you can!"[38] She had friends in high places.

Hanna never returned to Test Command 16. Wolfgang Spaete later wrote, "We assumed that she had gone to General v. Greim on the front to improve morale."[35]

After convalescing for a year and a half with a shattered back, Heini Dittmar returned to the air in April 1944.[39] On 6 July 1944 he pushed an advanced version of the Me 163B to 1,130 kilometers per hour (702 miles per hour), a new speed record, yet still shy of the sound barrier.[40] Dittmar was still the fastest man alive; but besides himself and his close associates, nobody knew and nobody cared. The events in the world around him dwarfed his achievement, made it a technological footnote, insignificant, overwhelmed by the horrors that were sweeping Europe and by the horrors yet to come.

The Messerschmitt 163B *Komet* does not rate even a footnote in most histories of the Second World War. A total of 364 Me 163Bs were built, with 279 intended for combat. Less than a quarter of these ever engaged the enemy. The Me 163B entered combat on 14 May 1944 with Wolfgang Spaete at the controls. Two Allied aircraft, possibly American P-47 Thunderbolts escaped because Spaete momentarily lost control of his aircraft at high speed.[41] In the months that followed, other rocket planes flew to the defense of the Fatherland. They and their pilots brought down about sixteen enemy aircraft. Allied fighters shot down six rocket planes, and bomber gun crews may have brought down a few more.[42] Counting bodies in a war is, at best, a haphazard business, but it is likely that the Me 163B, by virtue of its unstable fuel and unreliable rocket motor, killed more of its own pilots than did enemy airmen.

While at Bad Zwischenahn with Test Command 16, Hanna Reitsch had received an invitation from General Robert Ritter von Greim to join him on the Eastern Front. Greim was, at that time, in command of air support for the central sector of the front. His headquarters were near Vitebsk, several hundred miles east of East Prussia, halfway between what had been Germany's eastern frontier and Moscow.

Morale on the Eastern Front was, understandably, poor and getting worse. Since the disaster at Stalingrad a year earlier, the Soviet forces had been merciless in retaking their land. The German forces, overextended and undersupplied, could look forward to a long winter and their own destruction. Greim, according to Reitsch, felt that the presence of a much decorated woman from the Fatherland would inspire the troops and improve morale, if not their chances for victory. Probably Greim, with his precarious combat position, and Reitsch, after her disappointment with Test Command 16, would also have their morale boosted by a rendezvous at the front.

Reitsch arrived at Greim's headquarters in January 1944. (She remembered it as being in November 1943.) She found that she could not ignore the proximity of the war: All through the night, artillery rumbled in the distance. When the frigid dawn arrived, Reitsch and Greim flew closer to the front in a Fieseler *Storch* observation plane. They stayed at treetop altitude to avoid being seen by enemy aircraft. They landed near the German lines and transferred to an armored car, which carried them to a forward antiaircraft position.

No sooner had they arrived than the position was pounded by Soviet artillery. Everybody dove for cover. Soon the artillery shells were followed by bombs dropped from Soviet aircraft. The air was filled with the crashing of shells and the cries of wounded men. Hanna was at the center of the enemy's attack, and for the first time she felt the full terror of war. When the explosions at last ended, Hanna joined in tending to the wounded.

The next three weeks were much the same. Hanna flew to isolated outposts in Russia, dodged enemy fire, and talked with the sons of Germany about their grim situation.[43] Her encouragement from home was no doubt appreciated, but it was no substitute for supplies and reinforcements.

Reitsch and Greim would be together again soon, not because Reitsch journeyed to the front, but because the Soviet armies would advance to within striking distance of the Fatherland.

Whereas Hanna's visit to the Eastern Front had been intended to raise the morale of the Luftwaffe forces, her own morale deteriorated. Upon her return, her health once again failed her. She had contracted hepatitis, possibly facilitated by poor hygiene practiced by necessity on the Eastern Front. She was also depressed by the grueling living conditions of the German fighting forces in Russia and their hopeless tactical position.

She wrote of her mood at that time, "All I was certain of was that I believed wholeheartedly in Germany, my beloved country. Nothing—nobody—would persuade me to desert her."[44] Hanna's faith had shifted from God to Fatherland, from humble acceptance of God's blessings to a perverted patriotism in support of the Nazi cause.

Chapter 6

The Suicide Squadron

Hanna Reitsch's plan to deploy a squadron of suicide bombers lumbered along until the winter of 1943–1944 when it received a hearing from the Aeronautical Research Institute. At the conference, the plan was presented to technical specialists from the various parts of the munitions industries and representatives of Luftwaffe fighter and bomber squadrons. Surprisingly, the plan was found to be both technically and operationally sound, if not rational.

Two vehicles were considered as candidates for the suicide weapon: a piloted version of the V-1 buzz bomb, which would be deployed a half year later against England, and the Messerschmitt 328, a single-seat plane with a minuscule fifteen-foot wingspan, originally designed to be used as a fighter or light bomber. The Messerschmitt 328 was selected because it was already in production. All that was needed to begin construction and testing of the suicide weapons was approval from the highest authority in the Third Reich, Adolf Hitler.

The Fuehrer invited Hanna Reitsch to the Berghof, his mountain chalet above Berchtesgaden, on 28 February 1944. He intended to present her with a certificate formally awarding her the Iron Cross,

First Class even though she had received the award sixteen months earlier. This would be the first and only time that a daughter of the Third Reich would be formally presented with this high award. Hanna Reitsch was a heroine, and the Reich owed her a debt. She would try to collect on it, even though she had received it for making a sloppy landing in the rocket plane.

Hitler greeted Hanna in the big room that overlooked Berchtesgaden and the countryside below. He invited her to join him in tea. They were alone except for Colonel Nicolaus von Below, who was liaison officer for the Luftwaffe to Hitler. Hanna saw her opportunity in this relatively informal and private meeting, and she quickly outlined her plan for a "Suicide Squadron" to the Fuehrer.

Hitler listened, but he rejected the idea of suicide missions. In his assessment, the present situation was not serious enough to justify Germany's bravest pilots killing themselves in a desperate attempt to destroy the enemy. Besides, what would the people of Germany think if they knew their men were committing suicide? Public opinion would find the idea unacceptable. It was not the right psychological moment. Hitler reserved to himself the right to decide if and when that moment ever arrived.

Hitler then began to lecture Hanna on the numerous instances he saw in history of apparently hopeless situations that had been salvaged. Hanna found his examples irrelevant.

Hitler began explaining how the salvation of Germany would be brought about by jet aircraft. Hanna was a test pilot for the Luftwaffe, and she knew the potential and limitations of those aircraft. She felt that the Fuehrer was living in a fantasy world if he expected those aircraft to change anything. Finally Hanna lost patience and cut off Hitler in mid-sentence.

"Mein Fuehrer," she objected loudly, "you are speaking of the grandchild of an embryo."

Colonel von Below froze in horror. Hitler was dumbfounded. Nobody spoke to him that way. Not Goering, not Himmler, not any of his old cronies. Nobody. But here this zealot who barely came up to his chin, this brave little girl with the smashed face wanted to save Germany with mass acts of "self-sacrifice." Any man who behaved as she had might immediately find himself on a train to the eastern territories looking forward to permanent "resettlement." But Hitler let it pass, and Hanna kept on talking.

She talked about immediate solutions, and she did so in more detail than Hitler wanted to hear. It would take a long time for jet aircraft to grow up and become a force in any war, she argued. The Reich could build the Suicide Group now. The volunteer pilots were ready. All that were needed were the piloted projectiles and the organization.

Hitler crumpled under the onslaught. He would not at that moment approve of suicide missions, but he would approve development of the plane to be used, provided that he would not be bothered by Hanna or her group during the development of the weapons.[1]

Hitler reluctantly turned over the suicide projectile project to General Korten, Chief of the General Staff of the Luftwaffe. Korten assigned the project to *Kampf Geschwander* (Combat Squadron) 200, or KG200, which was responsible for specialized, audacious missions.[1,2]

Thousands of Luftwaffe pilots volunteered to die for the Reich, and seventy were selected to do so. Before being accepted into the "Suicide Group," volunteers were asked to sign the following statement:

I HEREBY APPLY TO BE ENROLLED IN THE SUICIDE GROUP AS PILOT OF A HUMAN GLIDER BOMB. I FULLY UNDERSTAND THAT EMPLOYMENT IN THIS CAPACITY WILL ENTAIL MY OWN DEATH.

Hanna signed the declaration immediately, but she put off actually joining the "Suicide Group," she said, "so as to avoid having to obey military orders."

During late winter and early spring of 1944, redesign and testing of the Messerschmitt 328 was done by the Reich Air Ministry. By April these tasks had been completed, and Hanna waited for a contract for the suicide weapons to be delivered to a factory in Thuringia. But, as Hanna lamented, the production never started and not a single operational Messerschmitt 328 was delivered.[1]

One report states that destruction of the factory in Thuringia prevented production of the weapon.[3] A more political reason is likely. Hitler never had any enthusiasm for the project, approving it only to pacify his troublesome heroine. Hermann Goering, chief of the Luftwaffe, had no enthusiasm for the project; and Major General Adolf Galland, Goering's Commander of the Fighter Arm of the Luftwaffe, thought it was a waste of effort and good pilots.[4] The project would die of neglect unless it could find a champion who had the influence within the bureaucracy of the Third Reich to make it happen.

Hanna Reitsch had begun to despair that her "Operation Suicide" would ever come into being when in April 1944 she received a telephone call from SS *Sturmbannfuehrer* (Major) Otto Skorzeny.[1] By virtue of one daring enterprise, Skorzeny had become a legend in Nazi Germany. On 13 September 1943 he led his team of SS commandos in the rescue of Mussolini from a mountaintop hotel in the Abruzzi mountains east of Rome. Skorzeny and over a hundred men landed in DFS-230 troop-carrying gliders in a rocky meadow adjacent to the mountaintop hotel where the deposed dictator was being held prisoner. Skorzeny and Mussolini were then passengers in an overloaded Fieseler *Storch* light plane that flew to safety from that same mountaintop meadow.[5] Skorzeny distinguished himself again on 20 July 1944 by taking a leading role in putting down the revolt in Berlin after the attempted assassination of Hitler.[6]

Skorzeny was a thirty-five-year-old Austrian. At six foot four inches and 220 pounds, he cut an impressive figure in his black and silver SS officer's uniform. He had a dark complexion with dark, wavy hair. His face might have been attractive had it not been marred by a dueling scar that ran from his left ear to the corner of his mouth and by an awkward attempt at a mustache that resembled the Fuehrer's.[7] He had been educated as an engineer, and he had been among the first of his Austrian countrymen to join the Nazi party. After the *Anschluss* with Germany, he volunteered for the Luftwaffe; but he was rejected because, at thirty-one, he was considered too old. Skorzeny joined the *Waffen* SS (Armed SS), his second choice, and led an undistinguished career for several years.

In April 1943 the *Waffen* SS General Staff offered Skorzeny the opportunity to form and lead a "special unit" that would take on important and dangerous projects that lay beyond normal military activities. It would exploit the technical wizardry of the Third Reich. It would be the SS's commando division.[8] Skorzeny weighed the offer against normal military life and threw in what he remembered as Nietzsche's advice: "Live dangerously!" Skorzeny took the advice and the job.[9]

As unlike as they were physically, Reitsch and Skorzeny shared a fanatical devotion to the Nazi cause, a casual attitude toward authority, and unconventional approaches to both the matter at hand and life in general. They became close friends and remained so long after the end of the war.[10]

Otto Skorzeny claimed that on a visit to Peenemuende in April 1944, he witnessed the launching of a V-1 and was immediately struck with the idea of increasing its effectiveness by having it guided by a pilot. Naturally, when he heard of Hanna Reitsch's plans for a similar weapon, he wanted to know more about it. Then he learned that she had proposed using the V-1 as a suicide bomb months earlier.[11] According to Reitsch's version, Skorzeny learned about the Suicide Group project from Heinrich Himmler, head of the SS, before seeing the V-1 at Peenemuende and contacting her.[1] Whoever had the idea first, they joined forces on the lunatic project in the spring of 1944.

Hanna paraphrased Skorzeny's approach to those who stood in his way as follows: "Hitler had vested him with full powers and had expressly called for a daily progress report." Hanna had failed to get the Reich Air Ministry's active support of the project. Skorzeny succeeded because he was a national hero, because he was a man, and because, he said, he had the Fuehrer's backing, which he did not have.

The standard version of the V-1 buzz bomb had a twenty-six-foot three-inch long fuselage with stubby wings at its midsection, which spanned only eighteen feet nine inches. An Argus As 014 pulse-jet engine perched over its aft section and tail. Its fuselage was filled with explosives, fuel, and a primitive guidance system. The job of converting it into a piloted suicide bomb was entrusted to the Henschel Company. In a period of fourteen days, Henschel converted the standard V-1s into four piloted versions, which were given the common code name "Reichenberg." The R-I version had a pilot's seat installed behind the wings, flaps on its wings, and landing skids. It had no engine and was intended as a training glider. The R-II version had two seats placed fore and aft of the wing. It was a training glider with dual controls for instructor and student. The R-III was similar to the R-I, but it had the standard pulse-jet engine perched just behind and above the pilot's head. It was an advanced trainer. The R-IV was the real thing: It had a single pilot seat, a pulse-jet engine, 1,874 pounds of high explosives in its nose, and no landing skids. It had no need for landing gear because, once airborne, it would not be coming back.[12,13]

Hanna Reitsch and Otto Skorzeny arrived at Laerz on a warm summer's day to observe the first test flight of the Reichenberg. The standard V-1 buzz bomb was normally launched from a catapult, but because it took off with a neck-snapping acceleration of over 17 g, a catapult launch was out of the question. The piloted version would be carried aloft slung under the right wing of a Heinkel 111 bomber, then dropped when it reached an appropriate altitude. The cover story used to explain the test flights to chance observers was that the piloted version of the V-1 was being used to study certain aerodynamic problems of the missile that could not be addressed by tracking from the ground.[12]

Reitsch and Skorzeny watched the Heinkel 111 passing 3,500 feet overhead. The Reichenberg, with a Luftwaffe pilot at the controls, was clearly visible under the bomber's wing. It was the R-III version, which had a single seat, an engine, and landing skids. Suddenly, the tiny aircraft was free. The pilot quickly pushed it to its top speed of 375 miles per hour, and the mother plane, cruising at 185 miles per hour, was left behind as if it were standing still. The flying bomb made a few wide circles; then the pilot pulled back on the throttle, reducing speed to land. He flew against the wind at a height of about 180 feet along the full length of the landing strip, then circled and came back again. This time he was only 9–12 feet above the ground, and everybody had the same thought: He's going too fast. Apparently the pilot thought so too. He pulled up and went around for another try. When he came back, he was still going too fast. As he reached the end of the field, he tried to pull up, but the belly of the tiny aircraft brushed the tops of the trees on a hillock at the end of the runway. Then it disappeared beyond the low ridge. Moments later two clouds of dust rose from beyond the hill.[11,12]

As most spectators watched the dust clouds in horror, according to one account, Otto Skorzeny was already planning the next flight.

"We'll need another pilot," he said to his aide. "Have him sign the release." Then Skorzeny walked to his Mercedes and drove away.

A Luftwaffe pilot who witnessed Skorzeny's cold-blooded reaction said, "Doesn't he give a damn that a man was just killed?"[14]

Nobody had an answer.

According to Skorzeny, he got into a half-track with two medical orderlies and sped to the crash site. Wings sheared from the body, the plexiglass canopy, and less recognizable debris lay everywhere. In the center of it all was the battered fuselage, which fortunately had not caught on fire. The pilot lay on the ground about a dozen yards from the body of the plane. He was alive but seriously injured. They sifted through the pieces of the shattered aircraft, but they could not find a clue to what went wrong.

The following day they launched another piloted V-1. The second pilot took his aircraft through a few more wide circles than did his unfortunate predecessor, then cut back the power and came in for a landing. He overshot the runway and crashed very near where the first pilot had crashed. The second pilot was also seriously injured, but he too survived. According to Skorzeny, "Hanna Reitsch could scarcely hold back her tears." Whether she was upset over the fate of the two pilots or the fate of her project is not clear. The Reich Air Ministry ordered an end to further test flights.

Two days later the two injured pilots were conscious and able to answer questions about their flights. Both made vague comments about vibrations in the joystick, but neither gave any worthwhile information about what had caused their crashes. Because no faults had been found with the piloted V-1 flying bomb, Hanna suspected the problem might lie with the pilots. She found what she was looking for in their personnel files: Neither had ever handled a really fast plane, certainly not one with as fast a landing speed as the V-1. They did not need to repair a defective weapon, Hanna concluded. They needed a pilot who could handle its high performance.[15]

"Ignore the ban," Hanna said to Skorzeny, "and I'll take the next one up myself."[16]

Skorzeny refused. "Listen, Hanna," he said, "if anything should happen to you, the Fuehrer will have me beheaded."[15]

"What!" Hanna shouted. "And they told me you were a soldier with the courage to disobey."[16]

Hanna was willing to follow Nietzsche's dictum, to live dangerously. The leader of the SS's commandos could do no less. Skorzeny told the station commander that the Air Ministry had verbally approved further tests.[15]

Hanna Reitsch was now under the plexiglass canopy of the modified buzz bomb. The Heinkel 111 dropped its cargo as planned, and Hanna fired the Argus As 014 pulse-jet engine. It came to life with a staccato rumble a few feet behind her head. Hanna pushed the tiny aircraft to its cruising speed. She took it through a few graceful turns, then brought it down toward the airfield for a landing.

Beads of cold sweat trickled down the back of Skorzeny's vulnerable neck as he watched the tiny aircraft approach the airfield at an incredible speed. Then the buzz bomb's skids were on the ground kicking up billows of dust as it slid across the field and stopped at the end of the strip.

They were all running toward her now, Skorzeny with them. It was fantastic; she had landed the flying bomb. She was safe. They lifted her out of the cockpit in triumph.

"Really stunning!" she said with delight, "it was really stunning."[15]

But Hanna's good luck with the Reichenberg was not to last. On one flight, Hanna's craft had just been dropped from the mother ship, the Heinkel 111, when Hanna heard a loud tearing noise. She struggled to keep the tiny aircraft under control, and managed to make a safe landing. An inspection of the Reichenberg afterward explained what had happened. A wing of the mother ship had grazed the rear of Hanna's aircraft just after its release. The tail had been torn and twisted about thirty degrees to the right. Only good luck and Hanna's consummate skill let her bring the damaged aircraft to a safe landing.

Not long after, Hanna was in the rear cockpit of the two-seat trainer version of the flying bomb, the R-II. She had had the ground crew wedge a sack of sand into the front seat as ballast to substitute for the absent student pilot. The aircraft was fueled, and Hanna was about to take it on a speed test run.

Hanna released the aircraft from the mother ship and fired its engine. The Reichenberg quickly reached its cruising speed of about 375 miles per hour. Hanna pushed the plane into a shallow dive, and its airspeed began to climb: 400, 450, then 500 miles per hour. When it reached 530 miles per hour, Hanna pulled back on the stick to bring the Reichenberg out of its dive. The stick would not move; nothing happened. The sack of sand in the front seat had shifted forward during the dive, and it had wedged itself against the controls. Hanna was wrestling with a sack of dead weight for control of her aircraft.

The unforgiving earth was rushing up at Hanna, prepared to punish her for her recklessness. She had to act quickly or die. She cut the engine to lose airspeed and thought of bailing out. Too late. She was too near the ground now, and she did not have the time. She pushed the stick forward. The nose of the aircraft dipped, and the sack of sand mercifully shifted again. Hanna pulled back on the stick, and it moved. The plane pulled out of its dive just before it hit the ground hard and fast. It skidded for what seemed forever, leaving behind it a trail of dust and debris. The hard landing had shattered the landing skids and splintered the body of the aircraft. Hanna opened the canopy and got out without a scratch.

On another day, she was again in the cramped cockpit of the flying bomb, tucked under the wing of an He 111. The ballast tank of the tiny aircraft had been filled with water to give it the weight of a fully loaded and armed flying bomb. Having reached an altitude of 18,000 feet above the endangered landscape of Hanna's beloved Germany, Hanna released her aircraft and began the test flight. She took it through its test maneuvers, then began to glide back to the airfield.

When she had dropped to 4,500 feet, Hanna tried to move the lever that opened the drain of the water ballast tank. It would not budge. It had been frozen in place by the cold air at 18,000 feet. The landing skids were not made to take the impact of landing the fully loaded aircraft. The weight of the flying bomb with its full ballast tank would shatter the skids and probably crush the aircraft and its pilot. Hanna clawed at the lever, trying to break the frozen plug free by brute force. The earth was reaching up for her, pulling her down for a final fatal embrace. She frantically worked at the lever till her fingers were bloodied; then, at last, a few hundred feet above the ground, the lever gave way and water gushed from the ballast tank. The last few gallons were still draining from the tank as the aircraft touched down and slid to a safe landing.

Hanna went up in the various versions of the Reichenberg nearly a dozen times and landed safely despite the aircraft's perverse tests of her piloting skills. When she had completed the test program, she began training instructors who would then teach the doomed pilots. Trainer and student were to fly glide tests in the two-seat version of the V-1. Hanna discovered that her students could fly the aircraft without difficulty, but the high-speed landings were another matter altogether. Training became a long and arduous task.[17]

By the time the program ended in February 1945, 175 R-IV piloted flying bombs had been built, and the first seventy pilots of the Suicide Group had been trained;[13] however, the prime targets had disappeared. As allied troops pushed the front into Germany, London and vital points in England fell beyond the flying range of the suicide bombs. Troop ships and beachheads were no longer points of vulnerability months after the continent had been invaded. The suicide pilots rejected one proposed target after another; the targets, they felt, were not worthy of their ultimate sacrifice for the Third Reich.

The Suicide Group was eventually disbanded, and its pilots returned to operational units.

Half a world away, high over the Pacific Ocean, Japanese pilots were taking action where their German counterparts had deferred. By the hundreds, *Kamikaze* (Divine Wind) pilots put their lives behind their commitment by crashing their own flying bombs into enemy targets. Though it was a losing battle, the Japanese suicide pilots destroyed dozens of American warships.

Chapter 7

Urgent and Special Missions

By mid-September 1944 the Soviet armies had advanced to within seven miles of Hitler's field headquarters at Wolf's Lair in East Prussia. Despite the proximity of the enemy, the Fuehrer was in residence, conducting the business of the Reich as badly as usual. SS Major Otto Skorzeny had been ordered to report there to attend briefings relating to the southern sector of the Eastern Front. The High Command, he surmised, had plans for him in that sector.[1]

Hitler had also summoned Luftwaffe Lieutenant General Robert Ritter von Greim to the Wolf's Lair in his frantic efforts to turn the advancing Soviet tide. Hanna Reitsch, whose involvement with the Suicide Squadron was diminishing, accompanied Greim as his confidante and pilot. Hitler had summoned him to solve a problem that was both strategic and personal. Hitler held his old comrade Hermann Goering responsible for the Luftwaffe's decline—never mind that Goering had created the Luftwaffe in the first place—and for the losses Germany was suffering at the hands of its enemies. Hitler needed Greim—or so he imagined—to retrieve the tottering Luftwaffe.[2]

Hitler had known Greim since the early days of the Nazi movement. They had met in Munich, and Greim had given Hitler his first airplane flight in 1920. The flight ended in a forced landing, which had soured Hitler on flying for many years.[3] Greim had shown himself to be the most loyal and selfless of Nazis. He was among the first to join the new Luftwaffe, and at the age of fifty-two, he was the Third Reich's oldest active fighter pilot.[2]

Hitler wanted to withdraw command from Hermann Goering. Like most of the senior officers in the Luftwaffe, he held his old comrade and collaborator in founding the Third Reich responsible for the air force's defeats. When they met, Hitler lectured Greim on Goering's many failures.[2] Greim wanted absolute control of the Luftwaffe. Goering resisted, wanting to retain control over personnel. Hitler was undecided.

Otto Skorzeny was walking down a garden path at the Wolf's Lair when, to his surprise, he encountered Hanna Reitsch. They explained to each other their reasons for being at Hitler's headquarters, and Hanna invited her commando colleague to join her and Greim at the "hut" they were sharing in the enclave.

Skorzeny arrived at the pavilion reserved for VIPs after midnight; the hour was not really late because the daily schedule dictated by Hitler started late and often ended near dawn. Hanna introduced Skorzeny to Greim in the living room of their accommodations, and soon the two men were discussing Germany's desperate situation. Greim saw one, and only one, slim hope. The Luftwaffe must bring into action a new weapon, the Messerschmitt 262 jet fighter, and with it regain air supremacy over Germany—if enough airplanes could be built, if enough fuel could be found, if the right tactics were used. Skorzeny was not optimistic. He knew that the Me 262 jet fighter had completed its flight tests two years earlier,[4] and only a small number had entered combat.[5]

In resolving the question of the leadership of the Luftwaffe, Hitler took the easy way out. He offered Greim the position of "deputy commander in chief" of the Luftwaffe. Even though he was still in command, Goering viewed Greim's appointment as a humiliation. Goering put off his new deputy by asking him to draw up proposals, which he would, no doubt, ignore. Goering showed his anger; and, as Hanna recounted, Greim "met with a terrific outburst from him."[2] Not surprisingly, both Greim and Hanna Reitsch viewed Hermann Goering as an incompetent, and they would soon call him a traitor.

In October 1944 Hanna Reitsch met Peter Riedel at the Flying Club in Berlin. Riedel was an old flying buddy who, with Wolf Hirth, Heini Dittmar, and Hanna, had charted the skies of South America more than a decade earlier. He was currently assigned to the German Embassy in Stockholm. Sweden was a neutral country, where the flow of information was not controlled as it was in Germany.

Riedel was upset, and he showed it when he threw a booklet down on a table in front of Hanna.

"If you want to know what's going on in Germany, look at this! This is what we find on our desks in the Embassy!"

Hanna picked up the booklet and quickly paged through it. It described the concentration camps, the gas chambers, and the final solution. Hanna was furious.

"And you believe this?" she asked her friend. "In the First World War, enemy propaganda smeared the German soldier with every imaginable barbarity—now it has come to gas chambers!"

Hanna's unhesitating, unequivocal response impressed Peter Riedel, although he was still not satisfied.

"I'll believe that from you," Riedel said; but then he asked Hanna, who was on good terms with Himmler, to confront him with the booklet immediately.

Hanna took up the challenge and called Himmler. He gave her permission to join him at his headquarters in the field.

When Hanna met with Himmler, she placed the booklet on the table before him, replaying the scene with Riedel.

"What do you say to this, Reichsfuehrer?"

Himmler picked up the booklet and paged through it dispassionately. When he had finished, he looked at Hanna without having changed his expression. "And you believe this, Frau Hanna?"

"No, of course not. But you must do something to counter it. You can't let them shoulder this onto Germany."

Himmler calmly returned the booklet to the table. Then again looking at Hanna he said, "You are right."[5]

As the Allies pressed their offensive, they made bombing raids against German cities a fundamental part of their strategy. The British bombed at night, and they made no distinction between military and civilian targets. The Americans bombed during the daytime, and, for the most part, focused on military targets. High-altitude bombardment was anything but high-precision bombing; and if a civilian area got hit, that was the Germans' problem. The Soviets approaching from the east had no concern for German military or civilians: They just wanted Germany destroyed.

The capital of the Reich was a prime bombing target. Hanna was back in Berlin in October 1944 when, while rushing to an air-raid shelter during an Allied raid, she was injured. She was whisked off to a Luftwaffe hospital, where she was diagnosed as having a torn capsule of the left elbow joint and a concussion. She was expected to convalesce in the hospital and not fly for several weeks. A few days after landing in the hospital, Hanna learned of the crash of a piloted V-1 during a test flight—the pilot had bailed out safely. Hanna went AWOL from the hospital, drove to the airport where her plane was kept, then flew to Laerz, where the suicide bomb test-flights were being conducted. When she returned to the hospital, the doctors grounded her, forbidding her to leave the hospital—or fly—until they discharged her.

Hanna was not concerned about her injuries. No bones were broken. The injury to her elbow would heal, and she still had a good right arm to control the stick of an airplane. The concussion? She had sustained a far more serious head injury before—the result of the crash landing of the rocket plane, the Me 163B—and recovered. And, if she had any pain, she had long ago learned to live with that. She could still live on the ragged edge. The worst that could happen would be that she would die a martyr for the Reich.

One can only wonder if Hanna's head injuries might have disconnected her higher cognitive processes, leaving her to be ruled by the primitive core of her brain, to be driven by her instincts: loyalty to her Fatherland and its Fuehrer, hate for Germany's enemies, and the adrenaline high of flying untested and dangerous aircraft. Was she like the boxer who had been on the losing end of too many matches, yet wanted to step back into the ring to prove that he still had it? Was she driven by an atavistic call for "honor" that sprang from the subconscious of the Third Reich and that would propel her through the final weeks of Nazi Germany's destruction?

While finishing her convalescence in the hospital, Hanna brooded over the vision of Berlin she had seen from the air and experienced on the ground. The city was being blasted into rubble by the Allied bombing. Worse destruction and suffering were to come; and Berlin, though Hanna did not express the thought in words, would inevitably fall. Hanna saw with remarkable prescience that, before the end, land routes into Berlin would be cut off. The city would be surrounded by its enemies and isolated. Its airports would be closed and the air above it filled with fire and smoke. She knew she would be there; she planned to be there. She would place herself at the ragged edge of rationality and fly into the inevitable Armageddon of the capital, once again gambling with death for the doomed Nazi cause.

During the winter of 1944–1945, Hanna began to plan a way she could serve the Reich by flying the wounded out of the capital and by flying what she described as "urgent and special missions." With the aid of an injured Luftwaffe colonel she met in the hospital, she began to map out routes to and from the center of Berlin and landings sites suitable for a helicopter, a craft similar to the one she flew indoors at the Deutschlandhalle in Berlin six years earlier. She systematically flew various approaches into Berlin, all at treetop level. When she could recognize all major landmarks and could find her way to the center of the city regardless of conditions, day or night, she knew she was ready.[6]

By the beginning of spring 1945 Otto Skorzeny was back in Berlin, conferring with the Nazi military leadership, cursing the conventional defenses the Nazi leadership was taking to hold back the onrushing tide of its enemies. Skorzeny learned that Hanna Reitsch, his friend and partner in the Suicide Squadron project, was also in Berlin; and he found her lying ill in a shelter.[7] (The nature of her illness has not been recorded.)

The war years had taken their toll on Hanna's health. In late 1940, she had spent three months in the hospital with scarlet fever. After her crash in the Me 163B rocket plane in the fall of 1942, she spent five months in the hospital and another three months recuperating after her release. After her visit with Greim on the Russian front in early 1944 she suffered from hepatitis. And in October 1944, she had entered the hospital again for several weeks after suffering a concussion in an air raid.

Despite her frail condition, Hanna intended to serve the Reich, if only by force of will alone. "I can still fly," she whispered to Skorzeny. "I can replace an airman. I shall soon be in the thick of it again."[7]

Through the grim winter of 1944–1945, as the Allies crossed over the German frontiers in both the west and the east, Hanna Reitsch did what she could to help the war effort, which was very little. Germany attempted to set up a barrier to the Soviets in the east, near Breslau in Silesia. Breslau was about sixty miles east of Hanna's hometown of Hirschberg, and she took the opportunity to fly as a courier between Berlin and Breslau.

In mid-April 1945 she made her third trip to Breslau, stopping first at Hirschberg. While there, she learned that she was not to fly on to Breslau. She said a melancholy farewell to her Hirschberg home; her family had long since evacuated to Salzburg in Austria. Hanna then flew to Kitzbuehel, Austria, 250 miles to the southwest. It was in Kitzbuehel that Hanna received an urgent message from Robert Ritter von Greim instructing her to join him in Munich for a "special task."[8]

Chapter 8

The Fuehrer's Bunker

Events unfolding in the capital of the crumbling Third Reich were a prelude to Hanna Reitsch's most terrifying flight, a journey of danger, madness, and death.

Friday, 20 April 1945 was Adolf Hitler's fifty-sixth birthday. His birthday had been celebrated as a national holiday since he assumed power in 1933, but there was no true celebration this day. As in better times, there had been a gathering in the Reich Chancellery of the leaders of the Third Reich: Reich Marshal Goering, Reichsfuehrer Himmler, Propaganda Minister Goebbels, Foreign Minister von Ribbentrop, Armaments Minister Speer, and Hitler's personal secretary Martin Bormann, and also Germany's military leaders, Admiral Doenitz, Field Marshal Keitel, and Army Generals Jodl and Krebs.[1,2] The mood of the day was at best melancholy. The decor of the Reich Chancellery contributed to the mood, because after Hitler moved into his underground bunker, the Chancellery's fine furnishings were packed away to protect them from damage during the constant bombings. Also, the Soviet army made its presence felt by its heavy-handed pounding at the door to Berlin.

After the formal reception, the Fuehrer went to the garden of the Chancellery, where he met with a delegation of Hitler Youth. They were children, actually, who had been fighting in the defense of Berlin. He then returned to his bunker for his daily military situation conference. At the conference, his commanding officers told him that the fall of Berlin was inevitable and urged him to escape to the south, where he could continue to direct the war.

Hitler answered, "I shall leave it to fate whether I die in the capital or fly to Obersalzberg at the last moment!"[1]

Hitler's cronies were more decisive. That evening, Heinrich Himmler departed for his headquarters in Hohenlychen to the north.[3] Albert Speer soon departed to Hamburg in the west.[1] Hermann Goering left for Obersalzberg in the south at the head of a truck caravan carrying the art treasures and war booty that had furnished his Berlin home, Karinhall.[2]

By 22 April even Hitler could see the desperate situation of Berlin. At the daily military conference, he blew up—some present said he had a nervous breakdown. The *Waffen* SS counterattack he had counted on never materialized, and the Soviet army was now within the Berlin city limits. Hitler cried that everyone had deserted him, that all was lost, that he would meet his end in Berlin.[2]

Although Hitler claimed to have been deserted, he did not expect to meet his end alone. Eva Braun had arrived from Berchtesgaden on 15 April,[4] and Hitler invited Joseph Goebbels, his wife Magda, and their six children to join them in residence in the bunker. Goebbels accepted the invitation.[2,5]

Word of Hitler's bizarre behavior soon reached General Karl Koller, Luftwaffe Chief of Staff, who was still in Berlin. Realizing that Hitler had already named Hermann Goering as his successor and grateful for an excuse to leave the doomed capital, Koller immediately flew to Obersalzberg to report to Goering.[6]

Hermann Goering had a legendary appetite for many things, including power. He moved to consolidate his political position with a telegram to Hitler; he sent a similar telegram to Foreign Minister von Ribbentrop, who was still in Berlin. In his telegrams, Goering cited Hitler's apparent abdication of leadership, and he advised them that if he did not receive instructions to the contrary by 10:00 P.M. of 23 April, he would assume the leadership of the Third Reich.

When Goering's telegrams arrived in Berlin, they were intercepted by Martin Bormann, who detested Goering and acted according to his own agenda. He presented to Hitler only the telegram addressed to von Ribbentrop, and accused Goering of attempting a coup d'état. This confrontation was followed by a mad barrage of telegrams: Hitler demanded Goering's immediate resignation of all offices for reasons of health. Goering replied that because of a severe heart attack, he was compelled to relinquish all his powers.[7] Martin Bormann ordered SS headquarters in Berchtesgaden to immediately arrest Goering and his staff.[8]

The following day, 24 April, Hitler ordered Robert Ritter von Greim, who was at the headquarters for *Luftflotte* 6 near Munich, to report immediately to Berlin. He gave no reason why Greim's presence in Berlin was required. Hitler also ordered General Karl Koller, who had by then been released from arrest by the SS, to come to Berlin. Greim planned to fly to Rechlin that night, then continue on to Berlin; but an air raid put his plane out of action before he could take off. Koller, who had left Berlin a few days earlier, saw Hitler's order as a pointless suicide mission. He refused to go.[9]

With his journey to join Hitler in Berlin delayed, Greim went to Obersalzberg to meet General Koller and, presumably, urge him to obey Hitler's order to go to Berlin. The meeting of Greim and Koller was, at best, awkward. Koller only wanted to argue Goering's innocence to his accusers; Greim labeled the Reich Marshal, his former commanding officer, a traitor. He told Koller not to defend Goering, but Koller persisted. He asked Greim to deliver to Hitler a full report, which he had written, recounting the events that led to Goering's fateful telegram and the subsequent accusations of treason. Greim accepted Koller's report and left Obersalzberg.[9]

During the day that Greim's journey to Berlin had been delayed, the isolation of Berlin had increased. The Soviet army won control of the last overland route to Berlin on the evening of 24 April.[10] The separation of the north and the south of Germany became a fact when the United States and Soviet armies met on the afternoon of the following day at Torgau on the Elbe River, seventy-five miles south of Berlin.[11] If Greim was to join Hitler in Berlin as ordered, he would have no choice but to fly, and it would be a very daring flight.

At about the time Hitler's cronies were wishing him a happy fifty-sixth birthday and preparing to desert Berlin, Hanna Reitsch was in her hometown of Hirschberg in Silesia also preparing to leave it. The Soviet forces had taken Breslau by then, and it was only a matter of

time before they would engulf Hirschberg. Most German civilians
had already left the vulnerable city. Hanna's parents, her sister Heidi
(who had lost her husband in the war), Heidi's three children, and
the family maid Anni had already evacuated to Salzburg.

From Hirschberg, Hanna flew to the vicinity of Kitzbuehel in Austria, where she had been given the task of inspecting emergency landing fields for hospital planes. Before starting this task, she stopped
off in Salzburg to meet with her family. After the happy one-day
reunion, she moved on to the resort community in the Alps to conduct her survey. It was there on 25 April that she received a message
from Robert Ritter von Greim to join him immediately in Munich.[12]

While on her way to Munich, Hanna learned that Greim had been
ordered to report to the Fuehrer in Berlin. Greim's request that
Hanna join him had a clearly practical aspect. With Berlin completely
surrounded by the Soviets and the invaders deep within the city, there
was no way to drive to the Reich Chancellery or even reach it from
one of Berlin's airports. Greim wanted Hanna with him to pilot a
helicopter on the final leg of the journey to the center of the city.[12]
She had become a public figure seven years earlier by flying the
Focke-Achgelis FW 61 helicopter in the Deutschlandhalle;[13] and during the recent winter, she had practiced navigating a helicopter just
over the treetops into the heart of Berlin with the thought that such
a flight might be needed sometime in the future.[14]

Greim, revealing his unique relationship to Hanna, also asked her
parents (presumably by telephone) to give their permission for her to
fly with him to Berlin. It was clear to all that the possibility of their
escaping Berlin was probably nil. Hanna's parents, revealing their loyalty to their daughter, the Reich, and Hitler, immediately gave their
approval.

On her way to join Greim in Munich, Hanna passed through Salzburg, arriving at midnight, for a last meeting with her family. She
said good-bye to her parents and embraced her sister's children as
they slept. Then she left for Munich.

At 2:30 A.M. on 26 April, Hanna Reitsch and Robert Ritter von
Greim took off from Neu-Bieberg, near Munich, in a Junkers Ju 188.
They would fly from airfield to airfield, the remaining islands of resistance in a bloody red Soviet sea. Their first stop would be the
Luftwaffe base at Rechlin, 60 miles northwest of Berlin, a little over
300 miles away. Hanna stood in the fuselage of the airplane, looking
out into the starry night. The enemy fighters that had dominated the

sky for weeks were nowhere to be seen. It was a good start for what Hanna expected to be a one-way trip.

They landed at Rechlin without incident at 4:00 A.M. where they were greeted with bleak news. Not one German airplane had been able to fly through the Soviet defenses into Berlin for two days. Even worse, the last helicopter at Rechlin had just been destroyed in an air strike. The only Berlin airport that was still under German control was Gatow, southwest of the city center. It was surrounded by the Soviet army and under constant artillery bombardment. Nobody knew if Gatow had enough undamaged runway left for a landing. They would try anyhow.

Greim decided to fly to Gatow as a lone passenger in a Focke-Wulf 190, the fastest aircraft available, and from there somehow make the final hop to the center of Berlin. The machine that would carry him was a single-seat fighter, which had been modified by the installation of a passenger seat behind the pilot's seat. The plane would be piloted by the same Luftwaffe sergeant who had flown Albert Speer to Gatow airport and then on to Berlin a few days earlier. Hanna had no desire to be left behind. Besides, she rationalized, she could navigate to the center of the besieged city at treetop level, having practiced doing so in the Focke helicopter.

As the pilot was preparing for the flight, and before Greim came to the aircraft, Hanna persuaded the pilot to let her be a passenger in the rear of the dark fuselage, wedged in with oxygen cylinders and other gear. She was unable to move or even see. Knowing that everything that was about to happen was outside of her control, she felt, for the first time in her life, terror.

Greim had already buckled himself into his seat when Hanna called out to him, revealing her presence. By then, it was too late to send her back; the plane was already bumping down the rough runway.

The second leg of their desperate journey began after dawn. Forty fighters roared off the ground from Rechlin, their escort on the thirty-minute trip to Gatow. The Focke-Wulf 190 raced down the runway, bumping over patched shell holes. Soon it was airborne; and Hanna tracked the progress of the flight the only way she could: She watched the luminous dial of her watch tick away the minutes.

By Hanna's reckoning, they were approaching their destination when the expected happened. Enemy planes, which were on constant patrol over Berlin, spotted the formation and attacked. The Focke-Wulf 190 went into a dive. Hanna was falling head first, trapped in the dark fuselage, unable to move. Hanna thought the plane had been hit. It was rocketing down to the earth where their lives would end abruptly in a smoking hole amid twisted metal and flame; but the pilot pulled the plane out of the dive. Soon after, they landed at Berlin's Gatow airport. Their escort had stayed aloft to do battle with the Russian fighters. Half of the forty escort planes were lost in the engagement.

When the Focke-Wulf 190 came to a stop, it had bullet holes in both of its wings. but the pilot and passengers were unharmed. They sprinted to the control officer's air-raid shelter, where Greim tried to get through to the Reich Chancellery by telephone. Finally, Colonel von Below was on the line. Until a few days earlier, he had been Goering's liaison officer with the Fuehrer, but now his loyalty was quickly shifting to Greim. Hitler wished to speak to Greim at all costs, von Below said, but he did not give a reason. Greim wanted to know if he and his companion, Hanna Reitsch, could get to the Chancellery by driving over land.

It was impossible, von Below said. All roads leading into Berlin had been cut by the Russians. The safest way into Berlin was to fly.

Greim would go to the inner city of Berlin. It was his duty as a German officer to obey his Fuehrer's order. He decided to fly a Fieseler *Storch*, a single-engine, high-wing light plane, just as Speer had done days earlier. Greim appropriated a plane, but Russian artillery fire smashed it just before they were to start. The last remaining *Storch* at Gatow was not ready for flight until almost 6:00 P.M. Greim insisted on piloting the plane; after all, he was experienced in flying under fire, whereas Hanna was not. She would ride behind him in the passenger's seat during the short hop into the city center.

Greim lifted off smoothly and flew at treetop height straight for the center of Berlin. They hoped to sneak through in the fading light, unseen by the enemy flying above and on the ground below. Their luck ran out. As they reached the Grunewald, Russian fighters appeared above. Ground troops also spotted them and began firing with everything they had. Rifles, machine guns, and antitank guns belched flame and bullets from the ground. The air around the tiny aircraft exploded in deadly puffs.

A bright yellow flame smashed through the plane, and Greim screamed that he was hit. He was bleeding, fainting, and their airplane was out of control. Hanna reached over Greim's unconscious body and grabbed the control stick. Shells exploded around them, and the

Storch was hit again. Hanna struggled with the plane, zigzagging it through the ground fire just above the treetops. Then the plane was hit again. Hanna watched with fear as gasoline poured out through bullet holes punched in both wing tanks, expecting an explosion at any second.

Hanna flew on toward the center of Berlin, and the ground fire slowly faded behind her. The ground below, she thought, must still be held by German troops. She got her bearings on familiar landmarks and flew straight for the broad, shrapnel-strewn East–West Axis. She brought the crippled Fieseler *Storch* to a safe landing just short of the Brandenburg Gate.

Greim was conscious again. His right foot had been shattered, smashed through by an armor-piercing bullet. Hanna tore a sleeve from her blouse and wrapped it tightly around Greim's leg to stop the bleeding from his wound. She struggled to get him out of the airplane, and when she did, they found themselves alone amid rubble and smoke at the center of a lifeless, bombed-out city. They could only hope that someone would come by to help them and pray that it would not be the Russians. Time dragged by, and at last a German truck pulled up and took them to the Reich Chancellery.[15]

Greim was carried on a stretcher down into the bunker by SS guards with Hanna close at hand. As they entered the bunker, they were greeted by Magda Goebbels, wife of the Minister of Propaganda. Though they had never met, Joseph Goebbels' wife embraced Hanna. She was amazed and impressed that anybody would have the loyalty and courage to come to Hitler in his final days of crisis. Greim was carried to the operating room of the Reich Chancellery where Hitler's personal surgeon, Dr. Stumpfegger, attended to his wound.[16,17]

Adolf Hitler came into Greim's sickroom to greet the injured general and Hanna Reitsch.[17] Hanna noticed that the Fuehrer's physical condition had seriously deteriorated.[16] The Fuehrer's condition had been worsening for several years, but the stress and his confinement to the bunker in the final months seemed to have accelerated his decline. His head drooped on his shoulders, and his eyes seemed sunken and glazed. His hands twitched continually, and he used his right to steady the left. When he walked, he shuffled, leaning to the left. When he stood, he was inclined to brace his left leg against a table for support.[16,18] Two doctors who saw him near the end diagnosed Parkinson's disease.[18] He also may have been a cocaine addict.[19] His mood went through wild swings; and although it cannot be proved, his disposition may have been the result of drug consumption as much as due to turbulent events.

Greim described for Hitler the long journey to the Reich Chancellery. When he finished, Hitler seized both hands of his loyal general. Then turning to Hanna Reitsch, he said, "Brave woman! So there is still some loyalty and courage left in this world!"[16]

"Do you know why I called you?" Hitler asked General Greim.

"No, mein Fuehrer."

"Because Hermann Goering has betrayed and deserted both me and his Fatherland. Behind my back he has established connections with the enemy. His action was a mark of cowardice. And against my orders he has gone to save himself at Berchtesgaden. From there he sent me a disrespectful telegram. He said that I had once named him as my successor and that now, as I was no longer able to rule from Berlin he was prepared to rule from Berchtesgaden in my place. He closes the wire by stating that if he has no answer from me by nine-thirty [*sic.* The telegram said 10:00 P.M.] on the date of the wire he would assume my answer to be in the affirmative."

Hitler's hand was shaking uncontrollably as he handed Greim the telegram that documented Goering's treachery. His face was deathly pallid, and it was twitching with rage as he damned Goering with explosive puffs of breath.

"An ultimatum! A crass ultimatum! Now nothing remains. Nothing is spared me. No allegiances are kept, no 'honor' lived up to, no disappointments that I have not had, no betrayals that I have not experienced, and now this above all else. Nothing remains. Every wrong has already been done me."

Hitler's eyes were half-closed yet hard, his voice unusually low. "I immediately had Goering arrested as a traitor to the Reich, took him from his offices, and removed him from all organizations. That is why I have called you to me. I hereby declare you Goering's successor as Oberbefehlshaber der Luftwaffe. In the name of the German people I give you my hand."

Hitler had appointed Greim Commander in Chief of the Luftwaffe and promoted him to the rank of Field Marshal. The mind-numbing lunacy of the wild journey and Greim's promotion escaped them all. Hitler had considered transferring Goering's control of the Luftwaffe to Greim seven months earlier but balked when Goering insisted on retaining his position. If Hitler wanted to put Greim in charge of the Luftwaffe when he finally stripped Goering of his powers, he could have done so with a radio message. He did not have to have his new Field Marshal crippled in a pointless flight to a doomed city. He did not have to waste twenty fighters and their pilots in the protection of Greim on the flight from Rechlin to Gatow. Furthermore, there was precious little of the Luftwaffe left to command. Most of its aircraft had been bombed and strafed into twisted junk, and little of what was left could get off the ground because of lack of fuel.

Somehow the madness of it all did not matter. Greim took Hitler's hands, and then Hanna did also. Greim was stunned by his appointment, and he and Hanna asked their Fuehrer for the ultimate privilege: to be allowed to stay in the bunker until the end. They wanted to atone for Goering's betrayal of the Fuehrer, the Luftwaffe, and the German people. They asked Hitler to let them, through the sacrifice of their own lives, save the "honor" of the fliers who had died, retrieve the "honor" of the Luftwaffe that Goering had betrayed, and redeem the "honor" of Germany before the world. Hitler agreed.

Like many Germans, Hanna Reitsch had a well-developed sense of honor for herself and for the Fatherland. Now, having joined the Fuehrer in his bunker, "honor" became her obsession.[20]

Later that evening as Russian shells fell above on the Chancellery, the structure Albert Speer had so proudly designed, Hitler spoke to Hanna alone in his quarters.

"Hanna," Hitler said, "you belong to those who will die with me. Each of us has a vial of poison such as this." He offered her two poison capsules, one for herself and one for her companion Greim. She took them. "I do not wish that one of us falls to the Russians alive," Hitler continued, "nor do I wish our bodies to be found by them. Each person is responsible for destroying his body so that nothing recognizable remains. Eva and I will have our bodies burned. You will devise your own method. Will you please so inform von Greim?"

Hanna realized that Hitler believed the cause was lost. She sank into a chair and said to him through her tears, "Mein Fuehrer, why do you stay? Why do you deprive Germany of your life? When the news was released that you would remain in Berlin to the last, the people were amazed with horror. 'The Fuehrer must live so that Germany can live,' the people said. Save yourself, Mein Fuehrer, that is the will of every German man."

"No Hanna," Hitler answered. "If I die it is for the 'honor' of our country, it is because as a soldier I must obey my own command that I would defend Berlin to the last. . . . By staying I believed that all the troops of the land would take example through my act and come to the rescue of the city. I hoped that they would rise to super-human efforts to save me and thereby save my three million countrymen. But, my Hanna, I still have hope. The army of General Wenck is moving up from the south. He must and will drive the Russians back long enough to save the people. Then we will fall back to hold again."

Although Hitler's words were full of hope, his face admitted defeat. He paced around the room with his hands clasped behind his back, and his head nervously bobbing up and down.[21]

Hanna took the vials of poison to Greim, and they joined the mass suicide pact of the bunker. When the end came, they intended to swallow the poison together. Then, just to be sure, each of them would pull the pin of a heavy grenade and hold it against their bodies in a final, glorious embrace. As the Fuehrer wished, there would be nothing left of them for the enemy to desecrate.

The Russian bombardment had increased in its fury. Heavy artillery shells were falling, shattering the once majestic buildings above the bunker.[21,22] The bunker was at least thirty feet below ground level with a sixteen-foot-thick concrete roof.[23] It was safe from any artillery shell or even the biggest bomb the enemy might want to toss its way. Berlin, however, was built on alluvial sand, which transmitted the effect of each explosion to the concrete sanctuary like a vibration shaking through jelly.[24] Residents of the bunker began to crack under the strain of the constant impacts, and here and there sobbing could be heard behind closed doors. Hanna spent the stressful night nursing Field Marshal Robert Ritter von Greim and, in her free moments, tracking down hand grenades to be used in their suicides.[25]

Luftwaffe General Karl Koller finally got up the courage to fly from Obersalzberg to Berlin as he had been ordered by Hitler. He arrived at Rechlin in the early morning of Friday, 27 April. He was prepared to fly to the center of the city as Speer and Reitsch and Greim had done earlier, but he was told it was impossible. Templehof airport had been taken by the Russians, and Gatow was now closed. Antiaircraft fire would be deadly. Koller, instead of going to Berlin, went to the headquarters of the Combined General Staff at nearby Furstenburg.

After talking to the ranking military officers of the Third Reich,

Koller telephoned the bunker to report to Hitler. When he was told
the Fuehrer was asleep and could not be disturbed, he spoke instead
to Ritter von Greim, telling him of his arrival. Greim advised Koller
not to attempt to come to Berlin. It was probably no longer possible
to get in or out. Koller sympathized with Greim's apparently hopeless
situation, with his injury, and his recent, pointless promotion.

"We shall not be able to work together for long, Herr Feldmar-
schall," Koller said, "we cannot make much of the Luftwaffe now,
and the end is approaching."

"Just you wait," Greim answered to Koller's amazement, "Don't
despair! Everything will be well! The presence of the Fuehrer and
his confidence have completely inspired me. This place is as good as
a fountain of youth for me!"

Koller was dumbfounded. In his inner monologue, he said, "The
whole place is a lunatic-asylum. I simply don't understand it. I often
ask myself whether I am really too stupid to follow the spiritual soar-
ings of these people and to recognize the way of salvation. Or perhaps
they have a sixth sense and can see things to which we ordinary mor-
tals are blind. One begins to doubt one's own sanity."

Not long afterwards, Koller received a telephone call from the bunker, from Hanna Reitsch. She wanted General Koller to carry a message back to her family in Salzburg, telling them once again, and for
the last time, that she could not have refused Greim's request that
she accompany him to join Hitler in Berlin. Hanna then launched
into an interminable—as Koller recalled it—description of her journey with Greim to meet Hitler in Berlin. By Koller's accounting, she
had gone on for twenty minutes before he cut her off. He reasoned,
he said, that Hanna was monopolizing the only telephone line into
the bunker; and it was needed for more-important business.[26]

The rising of the sun, the arrival of Koller, and the mad euphoria
they engendered must have given Reitsch and Greim the courage to
try the impossible. The Fieseler *Storch* they arrived in had, apparently,
been patched; and they went back to the roadway near the Brandenburg gate to attempt an escape from Berlin. With Hanna at the controls, they made two attempts to take off, but they had to give up
and return to the bunker because of the rain of artillery shells. The
tiny aircraft was finally destroyed during the bombardment the following morning.[27]

During the day of Friday, 27 April, Hanna was able to meet some
of the other residents of the bunker. Her favorites were the six chil-

dren of Joseph and Magda Goebbels. Twelve-year-old Helga was tall and intelligent; she had her father's dark eyes and hair. She was also his favorite. The prettiest of the group was Hilde, also a brunette; she was eleven. The only boy was ten-year-old Helmut. Holde was eight, a blonde little girl the others loved to tease. Six-year-old Hedde was also blonde. Heidi, the youngest, was not yet five.[28] To the children, the artillery shells exploding above were their "Uncle Fuehrer" conquering his enemies.[29] The children were not concerned about the battle going on above their heads; they were, in fact, delighted to be in "the cave" with their "Uncle Fuehrer." He had told them that his soldiers would soon drive back the Russians, and they could then go above ground to play in the garden.[30]

Hanna told the children long stories about the places she had been and her adventures in the air. She also taught them songs, which they sang for their "Uncle Fuehrer" and the wounded Field Marshal Greim.[30] She showed them how to fill the bunker of the doomed with the gentle melancholy of Tyrolean yodeling. Before they went to sleep, she sang to the children, "Tomorrow, and it be His will, the Lord shall wake thee once again."[31]

The patriarch of the clan, Minister of Propaganda Joseph Goebbels, was not nearly as pleasant company. He was the leading intellectual of the Nazi movement—if the terms "intellectual" and "Nazi" can be used together. He was ideologically cynical, a hater of the human race in general and Jews in particular, a theatrical orator, the quintessential liar of the Nazi cause, and devoted to Hitler. It is likely that Goebbels' perverse character derived, in part, from his own personal inadequacies. He was slight of build and had contracted polio as a child. This had left him with a crippled foot. He had thick black hair and the face of a weasel. In appearance, he was anything but the Aryan superman.[32] Nature had played many cruel tricks on him, and he had used the Nazi movement to pay back the world.

Goebbels lectured Hanna about his current obsession, Goering's treachery. "That swine," he said as he hobbled on his crippled foot, back and forth in his small room, "who has always set himself up as the Fuehrer's greatest support now does not have the courage to stand beside him. As if that were not enough, he wants to replace the Fuehrer as head of state. He, an incessant incompetent, who has destroyed the Fatherland with his mishandling and stupidity, now wants to lead the entire nation. By this alone he proves that he was never truly one of us, that at heart he was always weak and a traitor."

Goebbels turned to his captive audience of Hanna Reitsch and

Greim, and holding the back of a chair like a rostrum, continued his oration. "We are teaching the world how men die for their 'honor.' Our deaths shall be an eternal example to all Germans, to all friends and enemies alike. One day the whole world will acknowledge that we did right, that we sought to protect the world against Bolshevism with our lives. One day it will be set down in the history of all time."

Despite being caught up in the madness, Hanna was still perceptive enough to see that Goebbels was performing, as if for an assemblage of historians. But then, that was his job in the Third Reich, to give the official twist to the nonsense of the day and cloak it in imagined nobility.

Joseph Goebbels' last words to Hanna Reitsch and Robert Ritter von Greim still rang in her ears months later. "We shall go down for the glory of the Reich so that the name of Germany will live forever."[33]

Magda Goebbels appears to have been the perfect mate for the Minister of Propaganda. She would do anything to be near Hitler, even bear Joseph Goebbels' children and put up with his chronic infidelities. Her attitude toward her husband lay somewhere between reluctant tolerance and hate. The couple stayed together to preserve the image of the ideal family they presented to the people of Germany and because it was Hitler's will that they do so.[34]

"My Dear Hanna," Magda said, "when the end comes you must help me if I become weak about the children. You must help me to help them out of this life. They belong to the Third Reich and to the Fuehrer and if those two things cease to exist there can be no further place for them. But you must help me. My greatest fear is that at the last moment I will be too weak."[35]

Hanna's reaction to this mother's perverse plea for help is not recorded.

Hanna took particular notice of two other residents of the bunker, Martin Bormann, Hitler's personal secretary and right-hand man, and Eva Braun, Hitler's mistress. Hanna observed that Bormann spent most of his time "recording the momentous events in the bunker for posterity." His plan was that his account of the last days in the bunker would "take its place among the great chapters of German history." Eva Braun was, according to Hanna, beautiful but shallow. When not preening, she went about the bunker constantly whining, "Poor, poor Adolf, deserted by everyone, betrayed by all. Better that ten thousand others die than that he be lost to Germany."[35]

On 27 April, the Third Reich was crumbling like a sand castle in a rising tide. In the north, British forces were closing in on Bremen, and, to their west, a Polish armored division was nearing the sea southeast of the German naval base at Emden. Allied forces under the command of George Patton met Ukranian forces in Austria. In the south, French troops took control of the Swiss frontier and started securing the Black Forest south of Stuttgart. Nazi Germany no longer had the means or the will to continue fighting.[36]

The most-intensive artillery bombardment of the Reich Chancellery till then began on the evening of 27 April. Adding insult to injury, the Russians turned guns they had captured at Templehof airport to the south against the Chancellery.[24] The intensity of the shelling was felt in the bunker, and its residents were sure that Russian troops would overrun the Chancellery and be in the bunker very soon.

According to Hanna Reitsch, Hitler ordered a council of the group to review plans for their mass suicide. By now, everybody had a cyanide ampoule, and they went over the instructions for the proper use of the poison. They reviewed everybody's plans for the destruction of their bodies and calmly discussed which method would be most thorough. The suicide council concluded with everyone giving a speech about his or her loyalty to Germany and its mad Fuehrer.[37]

General Wenck's move from the south to retake Berlin stalled, his army defeated.[22] The defense of Berlin was now mostly in the hands of the Volkssturm, a ragged group of men too old to be in the regular armed forces, and about 1,000 Hitler Youth.[38,39] The rescue of the besieged city that Hitler hoped for never came. The Russian Army moved deeper into Berlin.

About 9:00 P.M. on the evening of Saturday, 28 April, one of Joseph Goebbels' assistants from the Propaganda Ministry ran from that building across the square to the bunker. He carried a transcribed copy of a Reuters news bulletin that had been broadcast in German by Radio Stockholm.[40,41] When Hitler saw the transcript, he raged like a madman.[42]

The broadcast said that Himmler had contacted Count Bernadotte of Sweden, with a secret peace proposal to be delivered to the American and British authorities. Himmler had requested that his identity be kept a secret during the negotiations. The Americans reportedly abided by his request, but the British did not.[42]

Hitler burst into Greim's room holding the transcript of the Stockholm radio broadcast and a map. His face was as white as that of a corpse. "Now Himmler has betrayed me. . . . You two must leave the Bunker as quickly as you can."[43]

In his subterranean world, detached from any reality, Hitler's self-pity had turned to self-delusion. He was sending a cripple, Field Marshal Greim, and his suicidal companion, Hanna Reitsch, on a mission to save Berlin and rebuild the Reich.

Hitler sat on the edge of Greim's sickbed. "Our only hope is Wenck, and to make his approach possible we must call up every available aircraft to cover his approach." Hitler talked of Wenck's artillery being heard pounding Russian tanks on the Potsdammer Platz, but it was more likely the sound of Russian tanks pounding Berlin.

"Every available plane must be called up by daylight," Hitler continued, "therefore it is my order to you to return to Rechlin and muster your planes from there. It is the task of your aircraft to destroy the positions from which the Russians will launch their attack on the Chancellery. With Luftwaffe help Wenck may get through. That is the first reason why you must leave the shelter. The second is that Himmler must be stopped." As he used the name of the traitorous Reichsfuehrer, Hitler's voice was unsteady, his lips trembled, and his hands shook.

"A traitor must never succeed me as Fuehrer," he told Greim. "You must get out to make sure he will not."

Greim and Reitsch protested that they could not reach Rechlin. They wished to die in the bunker with their Fuehrer.

Hitler answered, "As soldiers of the Reich it is our holy duty to exhaust every possibility. This is the only chance of success that remains. It is your duty and mine to take it."

"No, no," Hanna protested, "what can we accomplish now, even if we should get through? Everything is lost, to try to change it now is insane."

"Hanna," Greim said, "we are the only hope for those who remain here. If the chance is just the smallest, we owe it to them to take it. Not to go would rob them of the only light that remains. Maybe Wenck is there. Maybe we can help, but whether we can or cannot, we will go." Greim began to dress.

Hanna was sobbing. She refused to give up. "Mein Fuehrer, why, why don't you let us stay?"

The decision had been made. Hanna Reitsch was deprived of the honor of death with her Fuehrer in the bunker. "God protect you," Hitler said.[44]

Not counting the children, there were two kinds of people in the bunker: those who subscribed to Wagner's *Gotterdammerung* and intended to join in the cyanide communion with their Fuehrer, and those who, despite their sins, were still sane. One of the latter was SS *Obergruppenfuehrer* (Lieutenant General) Hermann Fegelein, Heinrich Himmler's liaison to Hitler. He had shown his knack for pragmatic action when, less than a year earlier, he had married Eva Braun's sister Gretl, who was pregnant, apparently by another man.[45] Until he found himself buried under the capital with a bunch of suicidal lunatics, his marriage had seemed to be a brilliant career move.

Fegelein had prudently left the bunker on Wednesday, 25 April, but his absence had gone unnoticed for two days.[46] He had imprudently been at his Berlin flat late in the evening of 27 April, where he was taken into custody by a small detachment of SS men.[47] What happened to Fegelein over the next twenty-four hours is not clear, but the denouement, precipitated in part by the news about Himmler, is known. Late in the evening of 28 April, Eva Braun's brother-in-law and Himmler's liaison to the Fuehrer was taken into the Chancellery garden and shot.[48]

News of the execution of Fegelein spread quickly through the bunker. Hanna learned of his fate before leaving it.[49,50] Word of her imminent departure with Greim also spread quickly. Everybody gave them quickly written letters to deliver to those who would live on. Magda Goebbels took a diamond ring from her finger for Hanna to wear in her memory.[51]

Thirty minutes after receiving Hitler's orders, Hanna Reitsch, Field Marshal Greim hobbling painfully on crutches, and Colonel von Below climbed out of the bunker and into hell.[51] The odor of sulphurous smoke was in their nostrils even before they reached the surface. They emerged onto the Vosstrasse, and found themselves surrounded by a sea of black smoke and yellow-red flames. The din of crashing artillery shells was all around them. SS troops were preparing to defend the Fuehrer's bunker from the final Russian assault.

Greim, Reitsch, and von Below commandeered an armored car and drove through the city, dreading the possibility that they might meet Russian troops at any turn. Shells were falling all around them; and several hundred yards short of their goal, their car was knocked out. They made it by foot to the Victory Column at the far end of the East–West Axis from the Brandenburg Gate. There they found that the Luftwaffe sergeant who had flown them to Gatow three days earlier was waiting to fly them out of Berlin in a two-seat Arado 96 trainer. The pilot and Greim got the seats, and Hanna once again rode behind them in the fuselage.

Russian-operated searchlights were crisscrossing the night sky as the tiny plane sped down the broad boulevard toward the Brandenburg Gate. It lifted off, and a few seconds later Hanna beheld the eerie sight of the stone monument, a dark silhouette frozen in the glare of searchlights. They climbed over the shattered city through the smoke and searchlight beams. An occasional tracer bullet flashed up from the ground, but none hit its target. The tiny plane and its passengers were soon in the dark shelter of a cloud bank.

They climbed through the cloud and emerged into the peaceful, heavenly beauty of a moon-lit sky. Below them, the cloud bank was a fleecy white blanket covering the flames and death far below. They flew west, over the province of Brandenburg, then north toward Rechlin. Through occasional black holes in the clouds, they saw the peaceful silvery lakes of Brandenburg as well as evidence that the war continued below. At first, the lights seemed to be bonfires. There were dozens of them, huge masses of flame billowing up from the fields below. The travelers soon realized that each bonfire was a village suffering the vengeance of the advancing Russian troops. Germany was in its death throes, but they flew on to Rechlin on their fool's errand to save the Reich when there was nothing left of it to save.[52]

Within minutes after Hanna Reitsch and Robert Ritter von Greim left the doomed bunker, Adolf Hitler began taking the final, decisive actions of his life. On behalf of his Fuehrer, Joseph Goebbels brought in a minor city bureaucrat who had the authority to perform marriage ceremonies. Under his officiation, Adolf Hitler married his longtime mistress, Eva Braun, in the small conference room, or "map room" of the bunker. The only others present at the ceremony were two witnesses, Joseph Goebbels and Martin Bormann. The brief ceremony ended shortly after midnight on 29 April. It was followed by a wedding breakfast with the other residents of the bunker.[53,54]

With Eva Braun finally having been made an honest and, ironically, happy woman, Hitler called upon his secretary to take dictation of his personal will and political testament. The latter document was filled with a final helping of forgettable Nazi rhetoric and the assignment of the blame for Germany's defeat and destruction to everyone but himself. The only item of political consequence it contained was the appointment of Grand Admiral Karl Doenitz as his successor as leader of Germany.[55,56]

The Arado 96 carrying Hanna Reitsch and Robert Ritter von Greim slipped through a screen of Russian fighter aircraft and landed in Rechlin, north of Berlin, about fifty minutes after leaving the capital. Greim immediately held a conference with his new staff, and he ordered all available aircraft to the defense of Berlin, fulfilling the first of the two orders given to him by Hitler.[57]

At about 4:00 A.M., the first light of dawn began to illuminate the smoke-streaked sky of Berlin. The last of the Luftwaffe forces—if they had in fact rallied to the aid of Berlin—were having little impact. The residents of the bunker below the Reich Chancellery paid little attention to the actions above them; they had their minds on other matters.

Sergeant Tornow, the trainer of Hitler's beloved Alsatian bitch Blondi, was roaring drunk. On Hitler's orders, he was in the bunker's toilet, which also served as a kennel, with Professor Werner Hasse, a physician who occasionally served Hitler. Tornow held open Blondi's mouth while Hasse placed a glass ampoule in the dog's mouth, then crushed it with pliers. The dog was dead almost instantly, having swallowed a fatal dose of cyanide. Moments later, Hitler came into the toilet to confirm that the poison, which he had obtained from the traitor Himmler, had been effective. He left a minute later not having said a word or betrayed any emotion.

Blondi had whelped four pups in the bunker sometime in March. Sergeant Tornow was responsible for them and several other dogs in the bunker. On orders, in a foreshadowing of terrors to come, he took his pistol and killed them all.[58]

Hitler and other officials inspected the destruction caused to a German city by Allied bombing in 1944. Hitler would soon retreat to his subterranean bunker adjacent to the Reich Chancellery in Berlin. Courtesy National Archives, photo War and Conflict # 1088.

Luftwaffe Colonel-General Robert Ritter von Greim was Hanna Reitsch's mentor and friend—many said her lover. Hanna accompanied Greim on an ill-fated flight into and out of Berlin in the final days of the war. Courtesy National Archives, photo no. 242–HBA–5377.

Hanna Reitsch, with Robert Ritter von Greim as her injured passenger, landed the bullet-riddled Fieseler *Storch* on the broad roadway leading to the Brandenburg Gate. Courtesy National Archives, photo no. 111–SC–423677.

The emergency exit of Hitler's Berlin bunker, at the right, led to the Reich Chancellery garden. The bunker was a popular tourist attraction when this photograph was taken not long after the end of the war. Courtesy National Archives, photo no. 111–SC–284970.

Minister of Propaganda Joseph Goebbels, Hitler's most strident and loyal crony, brought his wife and six children into the bunker, where they befriended Hanna Reitsch. Courtesy National Archives, photo no. 208–N–39233.

Heinrich Himmler, chief of the Gestapo and Reichsfuehrer of the SS, betrayed Hitler by attempting to arrange a separate peace with the Allies. Hitler sent Hanna Reitsch and Greim from Berlin on a doomed mission to stop the traitor Himmler. Courtesy National Archives, photo no. 226–P–25–1406.

Life goes on. After the war, Hanna Reitsch returned to her first joy, flying gliders. Photo circa 1956. Courtesy National Air and Space Museum, Smithsonian Institution, SI Neg. No. A 45979.

Europe: national boundaries, 1937; cities and locales, 1937–1945. Reitsch's and Greim's flight to Berlin on 25 April 1945 is represented by a dotted line. Reitsch and Greim's flight from Berlin starting on 28 April 1945 through 9 May 1945 is represented by a broken line.

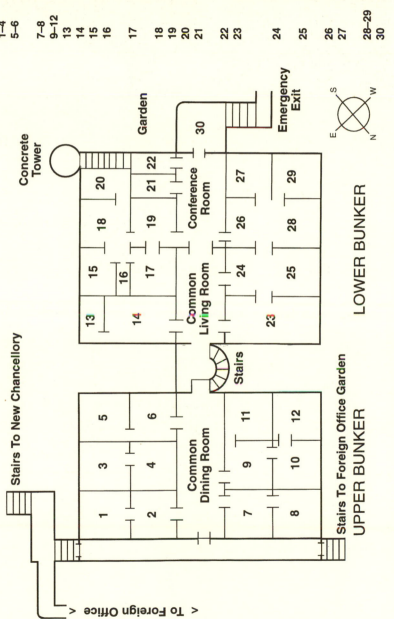

Floor plan of the Reich Chancellery bunker (Adapted from Trevor-Roper, p.108 and O'Donnell, p. 44).

Chapter 9

The Fools' Odyssey

Hanna Reitsch was at the controls of a Bucker 181, a small aircraft with good visibility, which carried her and Greim away from Rechlin. Following the second of the two orders they received from Hitler, they were in pursuit of the traitor Heinrich Himmler. They were on their way to Ploen, to the northwest, to the headquarters of Grand-Admiral Karl Doenitz, where they hoped to learn of Himmler's whereabouts.

The sky was swirling with Soviet planes and the last of Germany's planes; to stay out of the conflict, Hanna flew only one or two meters above the ground, avoiding roads and rail lines and taking advantage of the natural terrain to hide their tiny aircraft from the enemy. Despite Hanna's caution, the Bucker 181 was spotted and attacked twice by enemy planes. Reitsch landed at Lubeck; she and Greim would make the remainder of their trip to Ploen by automobile.[1,2]

Reitsch and Greim were still in Lubeck[2] when, a little after 10:00 P.M. on the evening of 1 May 1945,[1] Hamburg radio made the following announcement:

Our Fuehrer, Adolf Hitler, fighting to the last breath against Bolshevism, fell for Germany this afternoon in his operational headquarters in the Reich Chancellery. On 30 April the Fuehrer appointed Grand Admiral Doenitz his successor. The Grand Admiral and successor of the Fuehrer now speaks to the German people.[3]

Doenitz had no information about how Hitler had met his end, but he spoke of the Fuehrer's noble demise and the need to continue the battle against Bolshevism. Somehow the Grand Admiral had forgotten the Third Reich's motives and actions in pressing the war.[3]

However misleading the radio announcement was, it told Reitsch and Greim two important facts. Hitler was dead, and Doenitz was in command as successor: more reason to press on to his headquarters in Ploen.

Travel by automobile was as dangerous as flying. During their short road trip of about thirty miles, they had to pull to the side of the road to avoid being strafed. Hanna helped the crippled Greim find cover.[1,2]

Ploen was about sixty miles from the Danish border in Schleswig-Holstein. The ministers and military chieftains of the Third Reich who were still alive and able to reach it gathered there. Field Marshal Robert Ritter von Greim and Hanna Reitsch arrived there on 2 May. Greim's purposes were to obtain from Doenitz his orders on the immediate activities of the Luftwaffe and to fill him in on the details of Himmler's treason. Doenitz claimed he knew nothing of Himmler's ineffective attempt to negotiate an end of the war with the western Allies.[1]

Heinrich Himmler had arrived in Ploen the day before. Admiral Doenitz had already informed the Reichsfuehrer of the SS that there would be no place for him in the new government, but the SS chief was as hard to get rid of as an invasive cancer.[4] Doenitz was mindful of Himmler's former high position in the Third Reich and current control of the remnants of the SS. Despite Hitler's parting order to arrest Himmler,[5] Doenitz prudently tolerated him. The new head of state no doubt understood that within a few days, neither he nor Himmler, but the Allies would have control of Germany.

Next, Reitsch took Greim to nearby Dobbin to meet with Field Marshal Keitel to discuss air tactics that should be used to help General Wenck in his long awaited entry into Berlin. Keitel let Greim know that Wenck's army had long been destroyed or captured.[1]

Later that day, Greim was in conference with Doenitz and his ministers while Hanna waited outside. As Heinrich Himmler arrived late and uninvited for the conference, she confronted him, and later described the encounter.

"One minute, Herr Reichsfuehrer, A matter of the highest importance, if you can spare the time?"

"Of course." Himmler seemed to be in an almost jovial mood.

"Is it true, Herr Reichsfuehrer, that you contacted the Allies with proposals of peace without orders to do so from Hitler?"

"But of course."

"You betrayed your Fuehrer and your people in the very darkest hour?" Hanna was outraged at the man's impudence. "Such a thing is high treason, Herr Reichsfueher. You did that when your place was actually in the bunker with Hitler?"

"High treason? No! You'll see, history will weigh it differently. Hitler wanted to continue the fight. He was mad with his pride and his 'honor'. He wanted to shed more German blood when there was none left to flow. Hitler was insane. It should have been stopped long ago."

"Insane? I came from him less than 36 [sic] hours ago. He died for the cause he believed in. He died bravely and filled with the 'honor' you speak of, while you and Goering and the rest must now live as branded traitors and cowards."

"I did as I did to save German blood, to rescue what was left of our country."

"You speak of German blood, Herr Reichsfuehrer? You speak of it now? You should have thought of it years ago, before you became identified with the useless shedding of so much of it."

Himmler's reply was cut short by a sudden strafing attack that sent them both running for shelter.[6]

Doenitz's first war council, not surprisingly, resulted in very little that would help the current desperate situation of Germany. The new leaders realized that they were faced with the inevitable end of the Third Reich within days. Until then, the best they could do would be to hold back the Soviet armies, allowing as many civilian refugees as possible to flee to the west, where better treatment could be expected from the western Allies. To this end, Field Marshal Greim decided that he would return to his command in the south. En route, he would stop at Koeniggraetz, about 360 miles to the southeast of Ploen to meet with Field Marshal Joerner, who commanded troops in Silesia and Czechoslovakia.

Hanna Reitsch was again Greim's pilot. They left immediately for Koeniggraetz in a Dornier 217. The flight was apparently uneventful in that they successfully escaped attacks by enemy aircraft. They arrived in Koeniggraetz on 3 May; Greim immediately went to Joerner. Joerner told Greim that he had already ordered his troops to hold out against the Soviets as long as possible. Greim's and Reitsch's next task would be to deliver the same order of resistance to Field Marshal Kesselring at his headquarters in Graz, Austria.[7]

By this time, Greim's condition had seriously deteriorated. Several times during the flight to Koeniggraetz, he had momentarily lapses into unconsciousness,[7] and he was suffering from a severe case of nettel rash, possibly an allergic reaction that resulted from an anti-tetanus injection.[2] Greim entered the hospital for treatment. His mad hopscotch across Germany with Hanna Reitsch was interrupted for four days.[2,7]

On 7 May, while he was still hospitalized, news reached Greim that the surrender of Germany to the Allies would take place on the night of 9 May. He resolved to continue on to inform Field Marshal Kesselring of the impending capitulation and to confer with him on what orders to issue to the Luftwaffe.[2,7]

Hanna Reitsch was again at the controls of the Dornier 217. She flew the injured Field Marshal toward Graz, 250 miles due south of Koeniggraetz, to see Kesselring. The Third Reich had become a handful of besieged islands in a rising Red ocean, and the flight from one island to another was as dangerous as ever. Hanna evaded allied fighters, but she was less successful with German defenses. As she approached Graz, her aircraft was hit by German flak. She brought the severely damaged craft to a crash landing at the edge of the air-field. Neither Hanna nor Greim was injured beyond their existing conditions.[7]

Upon their arrival in Graz, Greim and Hanna Reitsch learned that Field Marshal Kesselring had withdrawn from Graz to the town of Zell am See,[7] 120 miles to the east and a similar distance from the advancing Soviet armies. Zell am See was deep within the Alpine Redoubt, a fiction created by the Germans but never prepared by them. Nevertheless, the Allies believed in it and would save its capture until the end.[8] The following day, 8 May, Reitsch flew Greim and herself in a reliable Fieseler *Storch* over the Alps to Zell am See in what she described as a "wonderfully peaceful flight."[2,7]

At Zell am See, Reitsch and Greim learned that the unconditional surrender of Germany was scheduled for midnight of 8–9 May. Though Field Marshal Kesselring was nowhere to be found,[7] they did locate General Karl Koller, chief of the Luftwaffe general staff. Koller was busy trying to arrange a dignified meeting between Hermann Goering and the American forces, who were sweeping over western Austria. He found Hanna and Greim, who was, by Hitler's directive, the new chief of the Luftwaffe and Koller's new commanding officer, an unnecessary complication in his efforts to put Goering in touch with the Americans.[9]

They seemed a pitiful apparition to Koller. Greim was on crutches feeling severe pain in his wounded right leg; his skin had turned a jaundiced yellow. He was a physical wreck. The preceding two weeks had also taken their toll on Hanna. She was an obvious emotional wreck, weeping as she refused to admit that the end was at hand. Both Reitsch and Greim denounced Hermann Goering. Greim threatened to have the former chief of the Luftwaffe shot; Hanna begged Koller not to defend him. Both Reitsch and Greim praised the Fatherland and its late Fuehrer.

Koller was appalled. "In these circumstances," he observed, "it is very difficult to discuss practical matters."[10]

Koller contrived to have his commanding officer, Field Marshal Greim, with his companion, Hanna Reitsch, transported to a hospital in Kitzbuehel, about twenty-five miles to the northwest. There, Hanna hoped to place Greim under the care of a well-known doctor who had recently opened his practice there.[7] They would be taken there by car in the company of a junior Luftwaffe officer.[9]

The junior officer was out of his depth in dealing with the two mad escapees from Berlin. On their way to the hospital, Greim ordered that the car be stopped. He stepped out into a field and tried to change into civilian clothes, a difficult undertaking for a man on crutches. Perhaps Greim, in his delerium, wanted to join in a fanatical resistance to the victorious Allies; possibly he wanted to disappear as an anonymous civilian into the peaceful Austrian countryside. The young officer managed to get his charge back into the car and on their way to the hospital only to be given an order by Greim that he was not inclined to obey. The young officer telephoned General

Koller to tell him that Greim wanted to be shot as a deserter, and asked what he should do. Koller ordered the young officer to deliver the chief of the Luftwaffe to the hospital despite his wish to the contrary.[9]

They arrived in Kitzbuehel on the morning of 9 May, and soon thereafter Hanna Reitsch and Robert Ritter von Greim met the American military authorities who had also recently arrived. The war and their odyssey in a futile attempt to save the Fatherland were over, but the madness had not yet played itself out.

Chapter 10

Choosing Life

June 1945, Kitzbuehel, Austria.

Spring had arrived in the Austrian Alps, bringing life to the mountain meadows. A woman visited a graveyard. There were many dead to remember. This woman was unique among those who lived through the Nazi era; she was one of a handful of women whose name and accomplishments were known beyond the frontiers of the Third Reich. Her name was Leni Riefenstahl.[1]

Leni Riefenstahl was a remarkably beautiful woman who had been a dancer, movie actress, script writer, movie producer, and director. In 1928 she had met Ernst Udet, Hanna Reitsch's mentor in the Luftwaffe, and they had become close friends. She had arranged for him to be a stunt pilot in a film she was about to act in, *The White Hell of Piz Palu*.[2] When Riefenstahl's talent as a director caught the attention of Adolf Hitler, he commissioned her to film the 1934 Nazi Party Rally in Nuremburg. The result was *Triumph of the Will*, a full-length masterpiece of political propaganda. The International Olympic Committee then invited her to film the Eleventh Olympic Games in Berlin in 1936.[3] The result was the classic *Olympia*.

While in the graveyard, Riefenstahl recognized another woman, small and frail, who was also known beyond the boundaries of Nazi Germany and whose exploits little more than a month earlier were becoming mythical in the unsettled peace after the war. The woman, Hanna Reitsch, was in the company of two American soldiers. Leni Riefenstahl engaged her in conversation.

As they spoke, Hanna took a crumpled letter from her pocket and handed it to Riefenstahl. "Read this letter," she said. "It may be taken away from me, and then no one but me will know what it says. It's from Dr. Goebbels and his wife Magda to their son Harald, who's thought to have been imprisoned by the Americans."[1]

The "letter" was actually two letters to Harald Quandt, Magda Goebbels' eighteen-year-old son from a previous marriage who was, at the time, in a prisoner of war camp in Canada.[4] The first four pages were written and signed by Joseph Goebbels, the remaining two by his wife Magda. Riefenstahl read through the wrinkled pages and was appalled by the strident compositions. She thought they were "bombastic in the extreme," and she sensed that Hanna thought so too.[1] Joseph Goebbels wrote:

28 April 45

Begun in the Fuehrer's bunker

My Dear Harald,
   We are now confined to the Fuehrer's bunker in the Reich Chancellery and are fighting for our lives and our honour. God alone knows what the outcome of this battle will be. I know, however, that we shall only come out of it, dead or alive, with honour and glory.[5]

Goebbels' reference to "honour" was an eerie echo of Hanna Reitsch's obsession with "honor" as noted by her interrogator.[6] Goebbels' words lumbered on in the ponderous rhetoric of his imagined *Gotterdammerung*, vainly trying to claim the moral high ground for the Nazi cause. He ended:

Farewell, my dear Harald. Whether we shall ever see each other again is in the lap of the gods. If we do not, may you always be proud of having belonged to a family which, even

in misfortune, remained loyal to the very end to the Fuehrer and his pure sacred cause.

All good things to you and my most heartfelt greetings
Your Papa[5]

Whereas Joseph Goebbels' letter was at best pathetic, Magda
Goebbels' letter to her son was terrifying:

28 April 1945

Written in the Fuehrer's bunker

My beloved Son,

We have now been here, in the Fuehrer's bunker, for 6
days—Papa, your six little brothers and sisters and I—in
order to bring our National Socialist existence to the only
possible and honourable conclusion. . . . Our splendid concept is perishing and with it goes everything beautiful, admirable, noble and good that I have known in my life. The
world which will succeed the Fuehrer and National-
Socialism is not worth living in and for this reason I have
brought the children here too. They are too good for the
life that will come after us and a gracious God will understand me if I myself give them release from it. . . .

. . . Everyone must die one day and is it not better to
live a fine, honourable, brave but short life than drag out
a long life of humiliation?

The letter must go—Hanna Reitsch is taking it. She is
flying out once more. I embrace you with my warmest,
most heartfelt and most maternal love.

My beloved son
Live for Germany!

Your Mother[7]

The children were those six lively faces that had brightened the
claustrophobic Berlin bunker for Hanna Reitsch.[8] It would be many
months before the basic facts were known, and decades before the
full story was revealed.

At about 5:00 P.M. on Wednesday, 1 May, after Hitler and Eva
Braun were dead and the Russians were closing in on the Reich Chan-

cellery, Magda Goebbels rounded up her six children and led them back to their room. She told her brood that they were to go to Berchtesgaden with their "Uncle Fuehrer." She fed each of them a chocolate candy that had been doped with a drug that would put them to sleep; she said the candies would "prevent air sickness." When the six children were asleep in their beds, Magda Goebbels brought out six of the cyanide vials that were ubiquitous in the bunker. She broke the capsules one by one into the mouths of her six children. The entire perverse act was accomplished in about an hour.[9]

Two and a half hours later, Joseph and Magda Goebbels climbed the stairway from the bunker to the emergency exit, which led into the rubble field that had been the garden of the Reich Chancellery. Magda Goebbels was the first to bite into a cyanide capsule. She sank slowly to the ground, then her husband squeezed the trigger of his Walther P-38 pistol, putting a bullet into the back of her head. Joseph Goebbels then bit into a cyanide capsule and a split second later fired a bullet into his right temple.[10]

Though Hanna probably did not feel any loss with the deaths of Joseph and Magda Goebbels, she seemed to be unable to see the "honor" in the murder of their six children, who were for a brief time her friends.

When Hanna left Berlin, she carried letters from others in the bunker in addition to those written by Joseph and Magda Goebbels. The fate of most of these letters is not known; however, Eva Braun had written a letter that she asked Hanna to deliver to her sister Gretl Fegelein. As with the Goebbelses' letters, Hanna had taken the liberty to read Eva Braun's letter. She described it as "so vulgar, so theatrical, and in such poor, adolescent taste" that its survival could only do harm to the memory of Hitler and the Reich. Interestingly, as Hanna remembered the letter, it made no mention of the execution of Gretl's husband, Hermann Fegelein, in the Reich Chancellery garden just before Hanna and Greim left Berlin. Hanna, who viewed Eva Braun as very beautiful but of a shallow mentality,[11] destroyed the letter.[12]

The two American soldiers who accompanied Hanna to the graveyard in Kitzbuehel wanted to leave. One of them took Hanna by the shoulder. She spoke to Leni Riefenstahl with a continued sense of urgency.

"I have to tell you one more thing," she said. "The Fuehrer mentioned you too; it was several months ago, when I finally managed to get to see him. I had to speak to him because I was the victim of the most incredible intrigues—having so many colleagues who resented my success. Hitler told me that this was unfortunately the fate of many women. He named several women and then said, 'Look at Leni Riefenstahl. She has so many enemies. I've been told she's sick, but I can't help her. If I did, it could mean her death.' "

One might have thought that Reitsch was showing her paranoia when she commented about "intrigues," but Leni Riefenstahl did not. The comment was a chilling reminder of a warning given her by Ernst Udet in 1933 soon after she had completed her first film on a Nazi party rally.

"Be careful," Udet said to her. "There's a group in the SA that's after your life."[1]

It was a credible warning. The SA, the "storm troopers," was a group of thugs who had been the organized muscle of the party. Its leadership had begun to challenge Hitler for control and threatened the order of the Party. On 30 June 1934, Hitler, with the backing of Goering and Himmler's SS and with the acquiescence of the German army, murdered the leadership of the SA, ending its influence in the Third Reich. Many more "intrigues" were to follow.[13]

Before leaving the cemetery, Hanna told Leni Riefenstahl about her plans for the suicide squadron and how Hitler had rejected the proposal. Hanna quoted Hitler, "Every person who risks his life in the battle for his Fatherland must have a chance for survival, even if it is small. We Germans are not Japanese kamikaze."

Riefenstahl wondered if Hanna had intended to be one of the suicide pilots, "Did you really intend to do that?"

"Yes," Hanna said with determination.

The American soldiers were impatient. There was nothing left to say. Leni Riefenstahl and Hanna Reitsch hugged each other, then Hanna returned with the soldiers to their Jeep. The two women never saw each other again.[1]

While in American custody, Hanna had tried to find a way to communicate with her family, who had relocated from Hirschberg in Silesia, which was now controlled by the Soviet army, to Salzburg. She was anxious to exchange news with them. Finally she found someone who was willing to carry a message to them. In response, she received the devastating news that they were all dead.

As Hanna explained it, as much for herself as for others, a rumor had been spreading in Salzburg that all refugees would be returned to their origins in what were then Soviet-controlled lands. Her father, a doctor, had seen the suffering handed out by the Soviet army when he was called upon to render medical assistance in regions temporarily recaptured by Germany. He feared the brutal treatment the victors would inflict on the women and children. "He had seen no alternative," Hanna said, "but to take upon himself the heaviest responsibility of all."[14]

In truth, he was less altruistic. The patriarch of the Reitsch family was an inveterate Nazi. In a grizzly parody of the deaths of the Goebbels family, he had used his rifle to murder his wife, his younger daughter, Heidi, Heidi's three children, and the family's faithful maid Anni. He then turned the rifle on himself.[1,15]

Robert Ritter von Greim, Field Marshal and the last chief of the Luftwaffe, friend, companion, and—many said—lover of Hanna Reitsch, followed the Reitsch family into death. Greim, his health wrecked, his air force destroyed, the Nazi cause and leadership discredited, and his country in ruin, had nothing to live for. While in American custody in Salzburg, on 24 May 1945, Greim made use of the poison capsule he had received while in the Berlin bunker. Hanna had agreed to follow him a week later so that they would be joined in death, but their deaths would not be linked in a suicide pact. The timing would protect their "honor."[16,17]

Hanna's American interrogator in Salzburg wrote his report with compassion.

> It is the opinion of the interrogator that the above information is given with a sincere and conscientious effort to be truthful and exact. The suicide [*sic*] of her family, the death of her closest friend, von Greim, the physical pain of Germany, and the trying nature of her experiences during the closing days of the war combined themselves to seriously tempt her to commit suicide as well.[18]

Did her courage fail her? Did she accept life, wretched as it was, as better than the oblivion of death? Who could say?

The whereabouts of Adolf Hitler were—at least among the western Allies—unknown. On 1 May, Admiral Doenitz had announced on German radio that the Fuehrer had fallen, a hero in the valiant defense of the capital of the Reich.[19] Though many may have believed he died, there was probably a good deal of skepticism about the circumstances. Within two days after Soviet victory in the battle for Berlin, the bodies of Hitler and the suicide and murder victims of the bunker had been found by Soviet intelligence. By mid-May, Soviet military staff in Berlin had told their western counterparts that Hitler's remains had been identified. Stalin was not convinced, and his men in Berlin began to backpedal. Soviet Marshal Zhukov told Dwight Eisenhower that there was "no solid evidence" of Hitler's death; a few days later at a Paris press conference, Eisenhower gave his opinion that the fate of Hitler was unknown. By summer, reports were surfacing that Hitler and Eva Braun had taken refuge in Spain, Argentina, the Swiss Alps, and a moated castle in Westphalia.[20]

As the surviving leaders of the Third Reich were being rounded up and their trials at Nuremburg being planned, the whereabouts of "War Criminal Number One," as the Soviets described him, were of great interest. Anyone who could shed light on the fate of Hitler was valuable indeed. As one of the last people to have seen him, Hanna Reitsch was kept in custody as a witness for the prosecution. Her interviewer summarized the value of the information she had to give:

> Her account of the flight into Berlin to report to Hitler and of her stay in the Fuehrer's bunker is probably as accurate a one as will be obtained of those last days, although the "is he dead or is he not dead" fate of Hitler is only answered to the extent of describing the mental state and the hopelessness of the last minute situation, from which individual opinions must be drawn. Her own opinion is that the tactical situation and Hitler's own physical conditions made any thoughts of his escape inconceivable.[6]

Still, nobody claimed to have the body or offered incontrovertible proof that Hitler was dead. The summary of Hanna Reitsch's interrogation was completed and dated 8 October 1945; it would later be published in supporting documents to the transcript of the Nuremburg War Crimes Trials.[21]

By September, the British Military Government in Germany had lost its patience with the rumors and obvious misstatements being circulated about Hitler. It commissioned an Oxford don, Hugh Trevor-Roper, to cut through the nonsense and piece together the truth.[20] On 1 November 1945, at a Berlin press conference, he pressented the essential facts, which, despite very few witnesses and a shortage of hard evidence, hold together till this day:

- Hitler married Eva Braun in the bunker.

- In the early hours of 30 April, both Hitler and his bride committed suicide.

- After their deaths, the bodies were taken to the garden of the Reich Chancellery, doused with gasoline, and burned.

- All stories of Hitler's escape from the bunker were found to be fabrications or without factual basis.[22,23]

There were, of course, more questions that needed answers than the whereabouts of Hitler. Someone who had been so closely acquainted with the leadership of the Nazi regime and who had been with Hitler so near the end might know something. Could Hanna Reitsch provide information about the crimes of Nazi Germany, and the guilt or innocence of its leaders? Just what did she know? And when did she know it? Her evidence could be used at the trials of those accused of war crimes to take place at Nuremburg. The victors could hold her until they had the answers.

According to Hanna, while she was being interviewed, she was given first-class accommodations, first in Kitzbuehel, then at a villa in Gmund. According to her interviewer, Hanna was in residence in a castle in Salzburg. Her story told, and with the War Crimes trials underway, Hanna was no longer of use to the Allies; yet they did not know if she might be needed to fill in some annoying gap, especially about the fate of Hitler. In October 1945 Hanna was shipped out of her finer accommodations to an internment camp where she complained about her tiny cell, the straw mattress on the floor, and the barred window without a pane of glass that let in the cool autumn air. She was later moved to another internment camp in Oberursel, near Frankfurt am Main. There, in August 1946, fifteen months after being taken into custody, she was released.[24,25]

One could not correctly say Hanna had been given her freedom. After all the terror and deaths and imprisonment, she was denied the one joy that might revive her strangled soul. Like all Germans after the war, she was prohibited from flying.[25,26]

Chapter 11

Return to the Sky

In the fifteen months Hanna Reitsch had spent in custody, many changes had swept over Germany. Though many Nazis were hiding in corners protesting their innocence, the Third Reich was gone. Its surviving leading criminals were about to receive their sentences at Nuremburg. With Joseph Goebbels, the master of the big lie, and his Ministry of Propaganda now an ugly memory, the press was free to print what it saw fit. To Hanna Reitsch's chagrin, what it printed was not always what she viewed as the truth. By word of mouth and in the press she was accused of having sexual relationships with Hitler (not likely), Joseph Goebbels (also unlikely, although he made it a matter of personal pride to seduce every attractive woman he encountered), and Robert Ritter von Greim (possibly, because they had a long and close personal relationship). According to the stories, she had been paid for her favors with a handsome life-style.[1]

One might speculate that Hanna was simply exhibiting a paranoia linked to the mental and emotional instability that overtook her at the end of the war. Yet if she were paranoid, she was not alone. Leni Riefenstahl complained of the same problems—which did not make it any better. The gutter press had also branded Riefenstahl as Hitler's former mistress.[2] Perhaps it was inevitable that both Leni Riefenstahl and Hanna Reitsch, possibly the two most interesting women produced by the Third Reich, should be linked romantically with the late Fuehrer. Eva Braun was a cipher, and the reality of her relationship to Hitler was too boring to be believed.

The gutter press, offensive as its stories were, could be discounted. Their stories would be remembered only until they were used to wrap dead fish. Professor Hugh Trevor-Roper was something else entirely. He was a respected Oxford don, and his book, *The Last Days of Hitler*[3] (published in 1947) became an international best-seller.

Trevor-Roper had taken his investigation into the death of Adolph Hitler, the results of which he had made public in November 1945, added new information as it became available, and presented it in book form.[4] It was immediately accepted as the definitive word on the subject. Trevor-Roper had no sympathy for Nazis, dead or alive, and he wrote with a very pointed pen. Hanna Reitsch was impaled on it, probably more so than other characters who passed through the Berlin Bunker in those final desperate days. His first words about her were a character analysis:

> There is a somewhat incomplete type of woman whose personal affections are (as the psychologists say) sublimated into abstract terms. When such a woman loves or hates, the object of her love or hatred appears to her not as a human being, but as a visible embodiment of some abstract quality. But since an abstraction is of necessity an inhuman, intellectual, and invariable thing, it can be the object only of narrow, concentrated, and uncompromising emotions: sympathy becomes religious adoration, detachment becomes theological hate. To this tiresome category of persons Hanna Reitsch belongs.[5]

Trevor-Roper followed this glib assessment—today it would be called sexist—with specific comments about her actions, relationships, and beliefs in the final days:

> Shrill, vain, and voluble, her character was well suited to that last subterranean madhouse in Berlin. An ardent Nazi, she had long worshiped at the shrine of Adolf Hitler; in

him, she says, she recognised the true quintessence of German honour, whatever that may mean. But later she discovered that she had made an error: Adolf Hitler's nature was more complex than she had supposed; it contained a certain quantity of impure and disastrous alloy; the true quintessence was represented by Ritter von Greim.[5]

Trevor-Roper cites as his source of information on Hanna Reitsch an interview of her published in the *News Chronicle* on 28, 29, and 30 December 1945,[5] which was, apparently, the report of her American army interviewer.[6] It is unlikely that he ever met her. Hanna was outraged; she denied any knowledge of the interview of her that formed a critical part of his book.[1] Nevertheless, Trevor-Roper's *The Last Days of Hitler* became a standard historical source, and nearly half a century after its initial publication, was released in its sixth edition.[7] History, as a cynic said, is written by the victors.

After her release from custody by the Americans, Hanna was, ironically, a displaced person, much like the Russians and Poles who had been conscripted into German labor camps and now found themselves without a home they could—or wanted to—return to. Hanna's home in Hirschberg, Silesia, had become part of Poland in the reordering of national boundaries that followed World War II. With the Third Reich and its various aircraft development activities out of business, and with her pilot's license revoked, Hanna was without a livelihood. She no longer had her family or Robert Ritter von Greim to return to. So, like the eastern European displaced persons, she stayed where she found herself when she was released in August 1946, in Oberursel. Understandably, she felt persecuted, depressed, and suicidal.[1]

One of the few survivors of those who had been close to Hanna was Otto Skorzeny, the SS officer who had been her partner in the suicide bomb project. Skorzeny had been acquitted of war crimes charges at a trial conducted at Dachau but was still being kept in custody by the Americans at the Oberursel interrogation camp. Viewing all of Germany as a prison, the Americans gave Skorzeny a Christmas parole. He visited Hanna in Oberursel before going to Munich to visit his family.[8]

Hanna's family, unlike Skorzeny's, was beyond her reach, buried near Salzburg, Austria. The new political reality rather than their deaths was the cause of their separation. In 1948 she attempted an illegal border crossing from the American-occupied sector of West Germany into Austria. She was arrested, fined, and released.[9]

With little else to do to occupy her time, Hanna Reitsch turned to writing her memoirs, which were published in 1951 as *Fliegen, mein Leben*.[10] (The English translation was published in 1954 as *Flying Is My Life*.[11]) The book tells of her life and pivotal events during World War II. She presents herself as a patriot, a loyal daughter of the Fatherland. Sadly, however, her autobiography is lacking in introspection or analysis of the moral consequences of her actions on behalf of the Third Reich. It makes no moral judgment of Nazi Germany or of Hitler and his court of criminals. It was an exercise in selective memory, rationalization, and denial. Perhaps this can be understood when truth is too painful to bear. Still, sales of the book gave her some income, which, with the generosity of her friends, allowed her to survive.[1]

By the early 1950s, that portion of Germany occupied by the western powers was evolving into the Federal Republic of Germany, or, simply, West Germany. With political autonomy returning, West Germany's pilots were again able to fly, and in 1951 Germany's glider clubs began to operate again. The following year they sent a team to compete in the World Gliding championships held in Spain, with Hanna as one of its members.[2] In 1953, as the sole woman competitor at the International Gliding Championships in Madrid, Hanna won the bronze medal. In 1957 she won the bronze medal at the German glider championships; and in the same year she also set two women's altitude records for gliders.[10]

Amid the renewed interest in flying gliders, Hanna found a need for her skills. In 1954 she went to work for the Focke–Wulf aircraft company as a test pilot of new gliders.[9] She was a pilot, and life was good again—or so she thought.

In 1958 a German glider team was to go to Poland to compete in the international gliding contest. Hanna was denied a visa. Although the Polish government never gave a reason for the denial, they may have still held a grudge against her because of her close association with Hitler. The incident was triply disappointing for her: She was denied the possibility of participating in competition; she was denied the opportunity to revisit her former home in Hirschberg, which was within the new boundaries of post–World War II Poland; and her teammates in the German Aero Club went on without her.

In a truly ironic twist of fate, the president of the German Aero Club at that time was Harald Quandt, the son of Magda Goebbels and stepson of Joseph Goebbels. When Hanna left the Berlin bunker, they had entrusted her with the two letters to be delivered to Quandt. Hanna had opened and read these two most personal letters and shared them with others long before Quandt knew they existed. Quandt stated that the refusal of the Polish government to grant Hanna a visa was a political matter, and he declined to become involved. He might have also been pleased to have this troublesome woman, who was a reminder of his painful past, out of the picture. Hanna felt that the German Aero Club's refusal to back her showed a lack of "honor." She resigned from the organization; and because it controlled all organized gliding activities in Germany, she cut herself off from her sport in her own country.[12]

With her back turned on Germany, Hanna ventured into international activities. Possibly the most significant of these was her friendship and association with Kwame Nkrumah, the first president of the west African republic of Ghana. Nkrumah, who was elected president in 1960, invited her to set up the National School of Gliding in Ghana, which she did in 1962.

One might think from this friendship that Hanna's personal zeitgeist had become liberalized, but a closer inspection reveals remnants of the pathology that led her to her friendship with Hitler. Nkrumah was a charismatic man with a vision of the unity and development of Black Africa, under his leadership and control. He quickly showed that his style of government was authoritarian. In early 1964 Ghana officially became a one-party state. Nkrumah built up his internal security forces and accepted the title of president for life. He became the center of a personality cult with his name ubiquitously gracing universities, landmarks, and public facilities.[13]

On February 24, 1966, four years after she arrived in Ghana, Hanna's stay abruptly ended when Nkrumah was deposed by the army and police. She recounted her experiences in her 1968 book, *Ich Flog für Kwame Nkrumah (I Flew for Kwame Nkrumah)*.

Hanna continued to fly, and she finally resolved her differences with the German Aero Club in 1978. She flew until a few months before her troubled life ended with a massive heart attack, at the age of 67, on 24 August 1979.[14] According to her wishes, she was buried in Salzburg, Austria,[15] near the family she tragically lost at the end of the War.

Hanna Reitsch never married or had children. Perhaps this part of her life is understandable. Where could she have found a man who was the match of Ernst Udet or Robert Ritter von Greim? How could simple domesticity fill her life when she had thrilled to flying at the razor-thin edge separating life from death? How could the obscurity of peace have compared with being the heroine of the Third Reich?

Aircraft Flown by Hanna Reitsch

Hanna Reitsch's achievement in aviation is that she flew—often as a test pilot—so many different kinds of aircraft. She piloted more aircraft than any other woman and more than at most a handful of men. The following is a list of many, though not all, aircraft she flew.

Gliders and sailplanes

- Grunau 9

- Grunau Baby

- Crane

- *See Adler* (the Sea Eagle glider seaplane)

- *Sperber* (Sparrow-hawk) Junior

- *Habicht* (Hawk)

- DFS 230 transport glider
- Messerschmitt 321 *Gigant* (giant)

Single-engine light planes

- Mercedes-Klemm
- Sport-Klemm
- Fieseler *Storch* (Stork)
- Messerschmitt Me-108
- Buecker 181
- Dornier 217

Bombers

- Dornier 17
- Stuka

Helicopter

- Focke-Achgelis FW 61 *Hubschrauber* (helicopter)

Jet-powered aircraft

- Reichenberg, Fi 103 (the piloted V-1 suicide bomb)

Rocket-powered aircraft

- Messerschmitt Me 163A
- Messerschmitt Me 163B *Komet* (Comet) interceptor

Appendix B

The Writings of Hanna Reitsch

Fliegen, mein Leben Stuttgart: Deutschen Verlagsanstalt, 1951; and Munich: Lehmann, 1976. (English translations: *Flying Is My Life* [New York: G. P. Putnam's Sons, 1954]; *The Sky My Kingdom* [The Bodley Head, 1955]; and *The Sky My Kingdom* [Novato, Calif.: Presidio Press, 1991].)

Ich Flog für Kwame Nkrumah (I Flew for Kwame Nkrumah) (Munich: J. F. Lehmann Verlag, 1968).

Das Unzerstorbare in meinem Leben (The Indestructible in My Life) (Munich: Lehmann, 1975).

Hoehen und Tiefen (Heights and Depths) (Munich and Berlin: Herbig, 1978).

Ich Flog in Afrika für Nkrumahs Ghana (I Flew in Africa for Nkrumah's Ghana) (Munich and Berlin: Herbig, 1979).

Notes

Note: Full bibliographical information for abbreviated titles of works can be found in the Selected Bibliography.

PREFACE

1. Joan Cook, "Hanna Reitsch, 67; A Top German Pilot," *New York Times*, August 31, 1979, page B-5.
2. *Koonz*, 3.

PRELUDE: HONOR

1. *Reitsch*, 227–28.
2. *NCA*, 551.
3. *NCA*, 552.
4. *NCA*, 571.

CHAPTER 1: SOARING OVER SILESIA

1. *Reitsch*, 3–4.
2. *Lomax WOTA*.
3. *Lomax FFTF*, 1.
4. *Reitsch*, 165–68.
5. *Lomax FFTF*, 4.
6. *Reitsch*, 17–18.
7. *Reitsch*, 5–7.
8. *Reitsch*, 8–11.
9. *Reitsch*, 12–16.
10. *Reitsch*, 17.
11. *Reitsch*, 19–21.
12. *Reitsch*, 21–24.
13. *Reitsch*, 25–27.
14. *Reitsch*, 29–31.
15. *Lomax WOTA*, 70–73.
16. *Lomax WOTA*, 76.
17. *Reitsch*, 33.
18. Erik Bergaust, *Reaching for the Stars* (New York: Doubleday and Company, Inc., 1960), 50.
19. Dennis Piszkiewicz, *The Nazi Rocketeers* (Westport, Conn.: Praeger, 1995), 19.
20. *Reitsch*, 38–42.
21. *Reitsch*, 34.
22. *Shirer*, 194–200.

CHAPTER 2: FLIGHT INSTRUCTOR TO TEST PILOT

1. John McClure Patterson, "At The Famous Wasserkuppe," *The National Aeronautic Magazine* (November 1933): 6–11.
2. D. S. Halacy, Jr., *With Wings As Eagles* (New York: The Bobbs-Merrill Company, Inc., 1975), 162–63.
3. *Reitsch*, 43–49.
4. *Reitsch*, 51–53.
5. *Reitsch*, 56–57.
6. F. C. Durant, III, "Lilienthal, Otto," in *The Encyclopedia Amer-*

icana, International Edition (Danbury, Conn: Grolier, Inc., 1993): Vol. 17, 478.

7. Special Correspondent, "Aerial Sailing in Germany," *Popular Flying* (October 1935): 374–75.

8. J. K. (Jack) O'Meara, "The 1931 Rhoen Soaring Contest," *Aero Digest* (October 1931): 48–49, 120, 122.

9. *Reitsch*, 58.

10. "Gliding As It Should Be," *Popular Flying* (October 1933): 399.

11. *Reitsch*, 59–61.

12. *Reitsch*, 62–64.

13. *Reitsch*, 65–66.

14. Halacy, *With Wings As Eagles*, 163.

15. Biographical file for Heinrich Dittmar, National Air and Space Museum, Smithsonian Institution. News articles in this file indicate that Dittmar was born in Schweinfurt, Germany, in 1911. He died, tragically, on 28 April 1960, while making the first test flight of a sportplane of his own design; it broke up in the air.

16. *Reitsch*, 69–74.

17. *Reitsch*, 76–78.

18. Halacy, *With Wings As Eagles*, 121–22.

19. *Lomax FFTF*, 24, 25–26.

20. *Shirer*, 282.

21. *Ethell*, 27–29.

22. *Reitsch*, 79–80.

23. *Ethell*, 21.

24. *Spaete*, 12–13.

25. *Wistrich*, 243–44.

26. *Reitsch*, 81–85.

27. *Reitsch*, 86–92.

28. *Reitsch*, 93–94.

29. *Shirer*, 283.

30. *Reitsch*, 95–108.

31. *Spaete*, 15.

32. *Reitsch*, 109–13.

33. *Reitsch*, 113–15.

34. *Reitsch*, 115–16.

35. *Wistrich*, 324.

36. *Lomax FFTF*, 86.

37. *Lomax FFTF*, 40.

38. *Lomax FFTF*, 38.

39. *Wistrich*, 105–6.

40. United States Army Intelligence and Security file on Robert Ritter von Greim obtained through the Freedom of Information Act.

41. Ernst Udet, *Ace of the Iron Cross* (Garden City: Doubleday and Company, Inc., 1970), 92.

42. *Reitsch*, 119.

43. *Shirer*, 297.

44. *Reitsch*, 121–27.

CHAPTER 3: THE IRON CROSS

1. *Reitsch*, 120.

2. *Reitsch*, 128–29.

3. *Reitsch*, 130–32.

4. *Lomax FFTF*, 54–55.

5. *Reitsch*, 131–35.

6. *Reitsch*, 135–40.

7. *Reitsch*, 164.

8. *Shirer*, 322–50.

9. *Shirer*, 420.

10. *Reitsch*, 141–51.

11. *Shirer*, 581–82.

12. *Shirer*, 597–99.

13. *Reitsch*, 169–72.

14. *Spaete*, 15, 81.

15. *Reitsch*, 174.

16. *Lomax WOTA*, 156.

17. *Lomax FFTF*, 76.

18. *Lomax FFTF*, 77.

19. J. R. Smith and Anthony L. Kay, *German Aircraft of the Second World War* (London: Putnam, 1972), 555–57.

20. *Reitsch*, 177–78.

21. *Reitsch*, 179–80.

22. *Reitsch*, 176.

23. *Reitsch*, 180–82.

24. *Reitsch*, 182–83.

25. *Reitsch*, 183–85.

26. *Reitsch*, 186–87.

27. *Koonz*, 3.

28. *Reitsch*, 28.

29. *Wistrich*, 342.

30. *Riefenstahl*, 30.

31. Roger Manvell and Heinrich Fraenkel, *Goering* (New York: Simon and Schuster, 1962), 261.

32. Manvell and Fraenkel, *Goering*, 418.

CHAPTER 4: THE ROCKET PLANE

1. *Ethell*, 29.

2. *Ethell*, 21.

3. *Ziegler*, 154.

4. *Ziegler*, 156.

5. *Spaete*, 15.

6. *Ethell*, 41.

7. David Masters, *German Jet Genesis* (London: Jane's Publishing Company Limited, 1982), 43–44.

8. *Ziegler*, 156–58.

9. *Ethell*, 44.

10. *Ethell*, 44–46.

11. *Ziegler*, 158–59.

12. *Spaete*, 25.

13. *Ziegler*, 159.

14. *Ethell*, 47–56.

15. *Spaete*, 62–63.

16. *Spaete*, 79–82.

17. *Spaete*, 115.

18. *Spaete*, 98–99.

19. *Ethell*, 61. This source gives the date of Dittmar's accident as November 1942.

20. *Ethell*, 89.

21. *Spaete*, 103–4.

22. *Reitsch*, 190.

23. *Ethell*, 56.

24. *Ethell*, 145.

25. *Ethell*, 148.

26. *Reitsch*, 192–94.

27. *Ethell*, 56–61.

28. *Spaete*, 104–5.
29. *Spaete*, 115.

CHAPTER 5: RECOVERY AND RETURN

1. *Reitsch*, 194–96.
2. *Lomax FFTF*, 94.
3. *Reitsch*, 196.
4. *Spaete*, 105.
5. *Reitsch*, 203.
6. *Shirer*, 932.
7. *Reitsch*, 196–98.
8. *Wistrich*, 101–4.
9. Albert Speer, *Inside the Third Reich* (New York: Macmillan, 1970), 178–79.
10. *Reitsch*, 199–201.
11. *Koonz*, 398–400.
12. Thomas Keneally, *Schindler's List* (New York: Simon and Schuster, 1982; Touchstone Edition, 1993), 252.
13. *Ethell*, 61, 65, 67.
14. Walter Dornberger, *V-2* (New York: Viking Press, 1954), 154.
15. Bergaust, *Reaching for the Stars*, 50.
16. Michael J. Neufeld, *The Rocket and the Reich* (New York: The Free Press, 1995), 101.
17. James McGovern, *Crossbow and Overcast* (New York: William Morrow and Co., Inc., 1964), 24.
18. Dornberger, *V-2*, 155–68.
19. David Irving, *The Mare's Nest* (Boston: Little, Brown and Company, 1965), 103–15.
20. Dornberger, *V-2*, 168.
21. *Reitsch*, 207–10.
22. *Ethell*, 78.
23. *Spaete*, 155.
24. *Ethell*, 71.
25. *Spaete*, 183.
26. *Ziegler*, 27.
27. *Ziegler*, 3.
28. *Ziegler*, 4–5.

29. Linda Hunt, *Bulletin of the Atomic Scientists* (April 1985): 16–24.

30. *U.S.A. v Karl Brandt, et al.*, as reported in "Extracts from Argumentation and Evidence of Prosecution and Defense; A. Medical Experiments," *Trials of War Criminals before the Nuremberg Military Tribunals*, Volume I, October 1946–April 1949 (Washington, D.C.: U.S. Government Printing Office), 92–198.

31. *Spaete*, 44–45.

32. *Ziegler*, 37–38.

33. *Spaete*, 155.

34. *Ziegler*, 39–40.

35. *Spaete*, 191–92.

36. *Spaete*, 99.

37. *Spaete*, 57.

38. *Spaete*, 197.

39. *Ethell*, 89.

40. *Ethell*, 101.

41. *Spaete*, 215–17.

42. *Ethell*, 144.

43. *Reitsch*, 204–6.

44. *Lomax FFTF*, 103.

CHAPTER 6: THE SUICIDE SQUADRON

1. *Reitsch*, 210–14.

2. David Irving, *Göring: A Biography* (New York: William Morrow and Company, Inc., 1989), 420.

3. *Lomax WOTA*, 159.

4. Irving, *Göring*, 428.

5. *Infield*, 37–45.

6. *Shirer*, 1066, 1068–69.

7. *Infield*, 2, 3.

8. *Infield*, 12–22.

9. *Skorzeny*, 13.

10. *Infield*, 146–47.

11. *Skorzeny*, 128–30.

12. *Reitsch*, 215–16.

13. Masters, *German Jet Genesis*, 52–53.

14. *Infield*, 10.

15. *Skorzeny*, 130–34.
16. Charles Foley, *Commando Extraordinary: A Biography of Otto Skorzeny*, (reprint), (Costa Mesa, Calif.: The Noontide Press, 1988), 105.
17. *Reitsch*, 217–18.

CHAPTER 7: URGENT AND SPECIAL MISSIONS

1. *Skorzeny*, 186.
2. Irving, *Göring*, 441.
3. *O'Donnell*, 152.
4. *Skorzeny*, 190–92.
5. Masters, *German Jet Genesis*, 117.
6. *Reitsch*, 220–21.
7. Foley, *Commando Extraordinary*, 148–49.
8. *Reitsch*, 221–22.

CHAPTER 8: THE FUEHRER'S BUNKER

1. Speer, *Inside the Third Reich*, 473–75.
2. *Shirer*, 1112–13.
3. *Trevor-Roper*, 115.
4. *O'Donnell*, 108.
5. *O'Donnell*, 112.
6. *Shirer*, 1115–16.
7. Speer, *Inside the Third Reich*, 482–83.
8. *Shirer*, 1118.
9. *Trevor-Roper*, 145–46.
10. *O'Donnell*, 139.
11. *Shirer*, 1106.
12. *Reitsch*, 222–23.
13. *Reitsch*, 135–40.
14. *Reitsch*, 220–21.
15. *Reitsch*, 223–28.
16. *Reitsch*, 229.
17. *NCA*, 554.
18. *O'Donnell*, 37–38.
19. *O'Donnell*, 317.

20. *NCA*, 544–55.
21. *NCA*, 555–56.
22. *Shirer*, 1120.
23. *O'Donnell*, 57–58.
24. *O'Donnell*, 144.
25. *NCA*, 556–57.
26. *Trevor-Roper*, 153–56.
27. Gerhard Boldt, *Hitler: The Last Ten Days* (New York: Coward, McCann and Geoghegan, Inc., 1973), 183, 188.
28. *O'Donnell*, 245.
29. *Reitsch*, 231.
30. *NCA*, 560.
31. *Reitsch*, 232.
32. *Wistrich*, 96–100.
33. *NCA*, 558–59.
34. *O'Donnell*, 126–28.
35. *NCA*, 559–61.
36. Various secondary sources.
37. *NCA*, 564.
38. *Shirer*, 1130.
39. *Trevor-Roper*, 143–44.
40. *O'Donnell*, 213–14.
41. *Shirer*, 1122.
42. *NCA*, 565.
43. *Reitsch*, 234.
44. *NCA*, 565–66.
45. *O'Donnell*, 102.
46. *O'Donnell*, 180.
47. *O'Donnell*, 195.
48. *Trevor-Roper*, 170–71.
49. *NCA*, 557.
50. *O'Donnell*, 211.
51. *NCA*, 566.
52. *Reitsch*, 235.
53. *Trevor-Roper*, 174.
54. *O'Donnell*, 157–58.
55. *Trevor-Roper*, 177–82.
56. *Shirer*, 1123–31.
57. *NCA*, 567.
58. *O'Donnell*, 164–65.

CHAPTER 9: THE FOOLS' ODYSSEY

1. *NCA*, 567–68.
2. *Reitsch*, 236.
3. *Shirer*, 1137–38.
4. Speer, *Inside the Third Reich*, 493–94.
5. *NCA*, 565.
6. *NCA*, 568.
7. *NCA*, 568–69.
8. *Infield*, 112–14, 116–17.
9. Manvell and Fraenkel, *Goering*, 234–36.
10. *Trevor-Roper*, 147, n. 173.

CHAPTER 10: CHOOSING LIFE

1. *Riefenstahl*, 319–21.
2. *Riefenstahl*, 67–69.
3. *Riefenstahl*, 168–73.
4. *O'Donnell*, 126.
5. Joseph Goebbels, *Final Entries 1945: The Diaries of Joseph Goebbels*, Hugh Trevor-Roper, ed. (New York: G. P. Putnam's Sons, 1978), 330.
6. *NCA*, 552.
7. Goebbels, 330–31.
8. *Reitsch*, 231.
9. *O'Donnell*, 257–61.
10. *O'Donnell*, 264.
11. *NCA*, 561.
12. *Trevor-Roper*, 172.
13. *Shirer*, 213–26.
14. *Reitsch*, 230.
15. *Reitsch*, 223.
16. *Wistrich*, 106.
17. *Lomax FFTF*, 135.
18. *NCA*, 571.
19. *O'Donnell*, 363.
20. *O'Donnell*, 369–70.
21. *NCA*.

22. *O'Donnell*, 371.
23. *Trevor-Roper*, 174–75.
24. *NCA*, 551.
25. *Reitsch*, 238–39.
26. *Lomax WOTA*, 163.

CHAPTER 11: RETURN TO THE SKY

1. *Lomax WOTA*, 163.
2. *Riefenstahl*, 328, 338–39.
3. *Trevor-Roper*.
4. *Trevor-Roper*, vii.
5. *Trevor-Roper*, 147–48.
6. *NCA*.
7. H. R. Trevor-Roper, *The Last Days of Hitler*, 6th ed. (Chicago: University of Chicago Press, 1992).
8. Foley, *Commando Extraordinary*, 177–78.
9. United States Army Intelligence and Security file on Hanna Reitsch obtained through the Freedom of Information Act.
10. *Wistrich*, 244.
11. *Reitsch*.
12. *Lomax FFTF*, 176.
13. "Nkrumah, Kwame," *The New Encyclopaedia Britannica*, 15th ed. (Chicago: Encyclopaedia Britannica, Inc., 1993), 8: 735–36.
14. *Lomax FFTF*, 221.
15. Joan Cook, "Hanna Reitsch, 67; A Top German Pilot," *New York Times*, August 31, 1979, page B-5.

Selected Bibliography

Abbreviations for the most often cited and important references are:

Ethell   Ethell, Jeffrey L. *Komet: The Messerschmitt 163*. New York: Sky Books Press, 1978.

Infield   Infield, Glen B. *Skorzeny: Hitler's Commando*. New York: St. Martin's Press, 1981.

Koonz   Koonz, Claudia. *Mothers in the Fatherland: Women, the Family, and Nazi Politics*. New York: St. Martin's Press, 1987.

Lomax FFTF   Lomax, Judy. *Flying for the Fatherland: The Century's Greatest Pilot*. New York: Bantam Books [paperback], 1991.

Lomax WOTA   Lomax, Judy. *Women of the Air*. New York: Dodd, Mead & Company, 1987.

NCA   Office of the United States Chief of Counsel
                      For Prosecution of Axis Criminality. *Nazi
                      Conspiracy and Aggression*, Volume VI.
                      Washington, D.C.: United States
                      Government Printing Office, 1946.

O'Donnell   O'Donnell, James P. *The Bunker: The History
                      of the Reich Chancellery Group*. Boston:
                      Houghton Mifflin Company, 1978.

Riefenstahl   Riefenstahl, Leni. *A Memoir*. New York: St.
                      Martin's Press, 1993.

Reitsch   Reitsch, Hanna. *Flying Is My Life*. New York:
                      G. P. Putnam's Sons, 1954.

Shirer   Shirer, William L. *The Rise and Fall of the
                      Third Reich*. New York: Simon and Schuster,
                      1960.

Skorzeny   Skorzeny, Otto. *Skorzeny's Secret Missions:
                      War Memoirs of the Most Dangerous Man in
                      Europe*. New York: E. P. Dutton, 1950.

Spaete   Spaete, Wolfgang. *Top Secret Bird: The
                      Luftwaffe's Me-163 Comet*. Missoula, Mont.:
                      Pictorial Histories Publishing Company,
                      1989.

Trevor-Roper   Trevor-Roper, H. R. *The Last Days of Hitler*.
                      New York: The Macmillan Company, 1947.

Wistrich   Wistrich, Robert. *Who's Who in Nazi
                      Germany*. New York: Macmillan Publishing
                      Co., Inc., 1982.

Ziegler   Ziegler, Mano. *Rocket Fighter*. Garden City:
                      Doubleday and Company, Inc., 1963.

Index

About the Author

DENNIS PISZKIEWICZ was educated as a scientist. He has taught college-level chemistry and biochemistry, and has worked as a scientist in the biotechnology industry. For many years he has been interested in the history of science and technology, and in 1995 *The Nazi Rocketeers* (Praeger) was published, a book about the men who developed the V-2 rocket in Germany during World War II. During his research for that book, he came across many references to a remarkable woman test pilot named Hanna Reitsch, who became the subject of this volume.